Clampdown:
Pop-Cultural Wars
on Class and Gender

Clampdown:
Pop-Cultural Wars
on Class and Gender

Rhian E. Jones

Winchester, UK
Washington, USA

First published by Zero Books, 2013
Zero Books is an imprint of John Hunt Publishing Ltd., Laurel House, Station Approach,
Alresford, Hants, SO24 9JH, UK
office1@jhpbooks.net
www.johnhuntpublishing.com
www.zero-books.net

For distributor details and how to order please visit the 'Ordering' section on our website.

Text copyright: Rhian E. Jones 2012

ISBN: 978 1 78099 708 7

A CIP catalogue record for this book is available from the British Library.

Design: Stuart Davies

Printed and bound by CPI Group (UK) Ltd, Croydon, CR0 4YY

We operate a distinctive and ethical publishing philosophy in all
areas of our business, from our global network of authors to
production and worldwide distribution.

CONTENTS

For T. (place) and T. (person)

There is a husky voice which I have often heard, and heard only there, among working-class girls of the rougher sort; it is known among the more 'respectable' working-classes as a 'common' voice.
- Richard Hoggart, *The Uses of Literacy* (1957)

There are in fact no masses; there are only ways of seeing people as masses.
- Raymond Williams, *Culture and Society 1780-1950* (1958)

INTRODUCTION:

THE GREATER ROCK'N'ROLL SWINDLE

'A given socio-historical moment is never homogeneous; on the contrary, it is rich in contradictions.'
– Antonio Gramsci

'Rock'n'roll is not just an important part of our culture... It's immensely important to the future of this country.'
- Tony Blair, 1994

The picture taken in July 1997 at a Downing Street reception, showing a rictus-grinned Tony Blair in conversation with a barely more at ease Noel Gallagher, provided an iconic illustration of 1990s music and politics in anxious accord. Its self-assured counterpart, a token of Britpop's compromised co-option, was the picture taken in September 2011 of Blur's former bassist Alex James playing far more relaxed host on his Cotswolds estate to not only David Cameron but also the tediously 'outrageous' conservative opinion-giver Jeremy Clarkson. As grim and unsurprising as the rat-king of government, media and police which the 2012 Leveson Enquiry uncovered, this interlinking of the boorish, the buffoonish, and the born-to-rule seemed to showcase a new presiding order as definitive as New Labour's had been. James's involvement with a plutocratic elite which Marina Hyde immortalised as 'the arseoisie' was a change from his Britpop days more in terms of setting than of attitude. In an interview on his retirement from the coke-and-champagne frontlines of Britpop and reinvention as a mock country squire, cynically shilling for both gentrifying lifestyle brand Daylesford Organic in liberal broadsheets and the fast-food industry in the pages of the *Sun*, James nevertheless declared politics 'just not my thing'.[1]

This book is a broadside aimed primarily at the ways in which class is represented and contested in popular culture, and how this relates to popular culture's oppositional potential. It is especially concerned with the intersection of class and gender representations in the figure of the working-class woman. Over the past twenty years, a queasy time of class confusion, class elision, and class erasure, neoliberalism has been asserted as strongly in British pop as in British politics. The treatment of working-class agency and identity in the cultural arena bears out the concept of popular culture as a critical site of contested hegemony. Indeed, given the alteration of the political and economic milieu over the past two decades, and the weakening hold of party and ideological ties as credible means of asserting opposition, the ways in which cultural space is occupied can hold as much if not more significance than the physical occupation of public space. A distinguishing mark of the 90s in Britain was a cultural shift from the nuanced and pluralistic articulation of identities to their appearance in a simulated or appropriated form, as stereotypes. Class, in particular, was reconfigured from an inherently political identity to one which could be temporarily occupied, communicated through signifiers which were increasingly abstracted, simplified, and stripped of meaning. Meanwhile, those who happened to be born with the same signifiers involuntarily bolted on were vanishing from public view, their place on the political and cultural stage taken by ersatz, commodified versions of themselves, in a process so seamless as to be sinister.

This book's first section surveys a series of contradictions in the ways in which the idea of a British working class is used in political and media rhetoric. The years since the 2008 banking crisis, and the subsequent imposition of austerity measures across Europe, have brought an overdue acknowledgement that, despite the suppression of class in political and cultural discourse, socioeconomic background remains a stubborn and strengthening line of division. Commentators on the left and right have referred to a 'crisis of working-class representation' in sites of decision-making power, which has been accompanied by a rise in political and media presentations of negative or mocking stereotypes of working-class identity, notably the 'chav'. While Owen Jones's *Chavs: The demonization of the working class* (2011) has provided the most prominent analysis of this, an increasing number of researchers and commentators are unmasking the hegemonic class hatred present in political and cultural depictions of 'chavs'. Relatively little attention, however, has been paid to an especially pernicious aspect of the 'chav' phenomenon: its use in promoting as beneficial or deserved policies on welfare, employment and reproductive rights which impact negatively on women's financial independence, sexual autonomy and social agency. Feminist commentators have criticized the impact on women of current government policy, but have been less explicit in connecting it with the concomitant onslaught of hegemonic stereotyping. This deficiency, partly the result of the unwillingness of mainstream liberal feminism to integrate a class dimension into its analysis or to broaden its academic, metropolitan and professional base of appeal, has coincided with the susceptibility of mainstream politicians, journalists and academics on the left and right to promote solutions rooted in reactionary or exclusionary ideals, leaving working-class women in a rhetorical and ideological blind spot.

Debates around 'chavs' are, of course, part of a longer tradition in which class is constructed, imposed and resisted through the use of signifiers and stereotypes. As a word, the meaning of 'chav' is impossibly contested, but as a specific idea, a commonly-understood stereotype, and an indiscriminate term of abuse for the poor, it has developed a peculiar and politically loaded edge. The combination figure of the 'chav' identified by Owen Jones, Imogen Tyler, and Beverley Skeggs, among others, is a negative reimagining of the worse off by the better off: a phantom, a scapegoat, a folk devil. But this spectre did not spring fully formed from the brow of David Cameron, James Delingpole, Martin Amis or Matt Lucas. Instead, its path into the popular imagination was smoothed by a variety of pop-cultural tendencies which, through their appropriative, pathologising and mocking use of working-class signifiers and identities, softened us up for accepting the making of the 'chav'. This book's central section looks at some elements of indie music in 90s and 00s Britain, tracing how forerunners of and variations on the 'chav' stereotype functioned to caricature and reconfigure class identity within it. Indie has, over the past decade, grown so uninspiring as to merit a succession of denunciations from within and without. These have focused variously on the abysmal quality of its 'landfill indie' variant, its alleged takeover by privately-educated nu-folkers, and its almost total failure to respond to an increasingly harsh rightwards turn in British politics; the 'death of the protest song', in comparison to the political engagement of musicians in previous eras, has become a cliché. What lies behind the draining of indie's oppositional energy is surely not especially surprising: indie was, in its Britpop mutation, fashioned into a hegemonic form of popular music, making it a site of struggle for representation, and 'indie' gained the ascendant in 90s Britain much as 'Labour' did, by accommodating rather than challenging the Thatcher-Blair consensus and becoming a travesty of itself.

Britpop's co-option by New Labour was enshrined, alongside similarly selected art, film, and fashion, in the spurious cultural canon associated with the Blairite brand of Cool Britannia. This process saw what was popularly perceived as 'indie' degenerate, from socially, racially, and sexually diverse, experimental, and relatively other, to increasingly homogenous, nostalgic, and confected. This development both reflected and reinforced a retrograde cultural climate, characterised by the rise of a commodified 'girl power' which emphasised empowerment through consumerism, a chauvinist and anti-intellectual backlash against progressive or politically-engaged cultural currents, and the fetishised appropriation of working-class identity, an agenda dictated by *Loaded* and the *Sun* as much as by the *NME*. Throughout the later 90s and the next decade, the industry and media concentration on bands conforming to a post-Oasis template set in motion a conveyor-belt of increasingly unimaginative and unreconstructed copyists. Among other negative effects, this process of greywashing divested indie of its earlier potential as a source of oppositional or emancipatory energy, especially for women. While what remains of contemporary indie has been subject to an emotional spasm regarding its narrow class makeup, its having 'gone posh', less if any attention has been paid to its gender bias or the resurgent chauvinism of which it is a notable exponent. After excavating the early 90s for more diverse and positive portrayals of female agency and identity, the book looks at how the 'chav' stereotype affects the presentation of women in the 00s musical mainstream, where women appear variously as appropriative chav-drag princesses, icons of insistently 'classy' nu-soul or nu-folk, or subjects of sensationalist proscriptive narratives, with a narrow subset of working-class women's experience exoticised and offered as a kind of stage-school burlesque.

The book's concluding section notes that the current crop of mainstream British musicians, while not uniformly posh, is certainly privileged, with the increasing homogeneity of its membership entrenching both a lack of wider class representation in the arts and entertainment world, and a lack of awareness or interrogation of this, in unfortunate concordance with the rise of an equally privileged political elite. It then considers whether 'chav' can be read as a positive, even radically oppositional identity, one which could suggest the intersectional power and potential of class as something

5

relevant and contemporary, beyond the current morass of stale, confected and appropriated class stereotypes. The purpose of this particular Britpop Revisited is not to compete with the abundance of other (more extensive, more impartial, more optimistic and more music-centred) retrospectives, but rather to situate aspects of it within broader political and cultural developments of the last few decades, and to examine how these tendencies have played themselves out. In order to meet the requirements of space and coherency, this overview highlights specific threads of a story among several, making it necessarily selective rather than exhaustive. There remains far more to tell than can be contained here. Race, in particular, which forms an obvious and significant intersection with class and gender in both the 'chav' debate and the contested construction of a 'British' identity, deserves a more in-depth analysis than I have felt qualified to provide. The point of articulating one among many neglected perspectives is not to suggest that popular music cannot be uncomplicatedly enjoyed, nor to posit some kind of classist conspiracy theory, nor yet to argue that music made by the comfortably-off cannot have merit. This book is, however, unavoidably and transparently informed by having grown up against a backdrop of Britpop and Blairism while uncomfortably aware of my place within a constituency and consciousness which fitted with neither. Written under few illusions and with fewer solutions to offer, this book is a tentative excavation of alternative political and cultural identities, revealing both what has been lost and what may yet be recovered.

PART ONE:

CLASS ACTS AND VANISHING ACTS

'Meanings of all kinds flow through the figures of women, and they often do not include who she herself is.'
– Marina Warner, *Monuments and Maidens* (1985)

'Are you disrespecting me?'
– 'Lauren Cooper', *The Catherine Tate Show* (2004)

Class, retreating and returning

The last thirty years have taken the concept of class on a curious journey, one which is difficult to fully comprehend without some idea both of class struggle and of what Stuart Hall described in 2011 as 'the long march of the Neoliberal Revolution'.[2] Based around the ideological championing of the free market and the demonization of the state as overweening and domineering, neoliberalism's trajectory over the past three decades has been characterised by the erosion of the postwar social contract, the increasing outsourcing and privatisation of the state's welfare functions, and a deepening divide between an increasingly precarious, insecure and impoverished workforce and a consolidated layer of the super-rich. The ostensibly opposed regimes of Thatcher and New Labour, the latter described by Hall as a 'hybrid' project composed of a dominant neoliberal strand and a subordinate social democratic strand, have both worked to further this project. The vocabulary of class struggle, however, has spent the same period noticeable by its absence from official discourse. Neoliberal 'end of history' propaganda, which asserted the implausibility of any narrative other than the continuation of capitalism, has been accompanied by the denial of diverging class interests, on the grounds that a working class no longer visibly exists in the manner associated with its formative struggles under industrialisation. A marked symptom of the rightwards turn of the 90s Labour Party under Tony Blair was the overt treatment of working-class consciousness as a shibboleth, not simply irrelevant but actively unhelpful in pursuing electoral success, and something which could expect short shrift in a modern and progressive Britain. While New Labour in government was of limited but undeniable benefit to working people, through the minimum wage, tax credits and increased public spending, the discourse which delivered these policies had no place for the idea of working-class as a positive identity. New Labour's acceptance of the post-Thatcher settlement – an annihilated manufacturing industry, tax cuts slanted in favour of the wealthy, a deregulated free market, demoralised and weak trade unions – was accompanied by its submission to an idea which can charitably be described as optimistic: that entrepreneurship and aspiration would inevitably see what remained of the working class raised to the contented ranks of the middle class, ignoring or denying structural and systemic reasons, based on frustratingly uncooperative material reality, which might hinder this. Academia, too, experienced a drift away from the discussion or exploration of class identity in cultural and media studies after the 80s, with the teaching and researching of issues of class inequality regarded as 'paranoid' and an embarrassment.[3]

When observing the ebb and flow of attention to class, however, it is clear that several paradoxes are at play. Firstly, the vanishing of analytical perspectives based around class occurred alongside a deepening of socioeconomic divisions. Since the rose-tinted social-democratic vistas stretching from the postwar settlement to the early 1970s, the wages of the middle and working classes have stagnated or fallen in real terms, exacerbated since the 70s by successive governments' pursuit of monetarist policies in thrall to the logic of the market. Attendant government commitment to tax cuts and the privatisation of state assets has enabled the income of the richest to climb to unprecedented levels, while much of the country remains in a state of post-industrial devastation, its population still bereft of secure and respectably-paid work. Twenty years after the miners' strike of 1984–5, research from Sheffield Hallam University indicated that less than half of jobs lost in coalfield districts had been replaced.[4] In the slice of south Wales where I grew up, the most substantial attempts at economic regeneration seemed to be the daffodils planted along the M4 corridor to improve the view for commuters. The UK's turn from a manufacturing economy based on mines, factories and shipyards, to a post-Fordist society characterised by the outsourcing of industrial labour and the spread of a service economy, has obviously and inevitably altered the subjective experience of the working class from what it was throughout the nineteenth and twentieth centuries. This has, in turn, destabilised the conceptual frameworks and analytical approaches to class inherited from industrial capitalism. However, it is equally obvious that those employed in retail work, call centres and customer service, in warehouses and offices and restaurants and shops and tourist attractions across the land, would still consider themselves as forming a distinct class, if a disorganised, alienated and powerless one. Moreover, the international economic upheaval unleashed by the 2008 banking crisis, an occasion seized upon by neoliberal economists, bosses and politicians as an opportunity for further privatisation, forcing down of wages and greater job insecurity, has accelerated the spread of precarious working from the margins to the core of the workforce and widened the gap between wage levels and the cost of living, making socioeconomic inequality far more difficult to deny.

As neoliberal rhetoric, whether the Blairite decree that we are all middle-class now, or the Coalition's more recent assertion that we are all in this together, has been increasingly contradicted by material reality, party-political attempts to reconstitute the idea of class, when they can be glimpsed, have been disappointingly informed by atavistic paternalism at best and disingenuous chauvinism at worst. In 2010, the conservative thinker Phillip Blond's Red Toryism, in essence a reboot of the 'shire Toryism' which still informs many of the party's rural traditionalists, sought to attribute the UK's ills to the combined effects of market individualism and a permissive counterculture, blaming the latter for the destruction of working-class family life and prescribing a back-to-the-village solution rooted in paternalist social relations. Red Toryism found a curious mirror-image in one aspect of the short-lived Blue Labour project, namely Maurice Glasman's presentation of the Labour party's history after 1945 as an emasculating 'cross-class marriage' of put-upon working-class husband and domineering middle-class wife. Similar sentiments informed the speech made in April 2011 by the Conservative minister David Willetts, in which he attempted to portray the advance of feminism, which among other achievements had enabled larger numbers of women to enter higher education and employment, as a process which had displaced and weakened working-class men. It should hardly require pointing out that this is disingenuous dog-whistling which criticises women's emancipation while offering nothing to address the very real disadvantages and anxieties of working-class men still affected by the economic trauma of the 80s. Furthermore, in pictures which postulate some disciplined army of empowered middle-class feminists against an incoherently resentful horde of disenfranchised working-class men, not only is the left's long history of intersectional cooperation ignored, but a group who should form a glaringly integral part of the picture – working-class women – are instead excluded from the frame entirely.

Chavs: the reworking of class

Despite insultingly obvious and deepening socioeconomic divides, official discourse still insists that we live in a meritocracy. From this, it follows that anyone unable to gain a sufficient share in the wealth – since they cannot be structurally disadvantaged – must simply not be trying hard enough. In order to reconcile this almost charmingly insincere mantra with the manifest reality of life after the credit crunch, with its falling wages, rising prices, and flatlining standards of living, Victorian and Edwardian ideas of the undeserving poor have been reanimated. Class is increasingly identified by moral rather than economic or occupational indicators, with class-inflected ideas of 'respectability' the means by which morality is made publically visible. Rejuvenated portrayals of an idle, stupid and semi-criminal underclass, 'disrespectable' and therefore immoral, make it possible for politicians and the media to present the economic position of these groups as self-inflicted and deserved, logically consistent with their lack of input and contribution to society. This idea is also logically consistent with the great switch of blame for the current financial crisis, from the incompetence, corruption and recklessness of banks and stockbrokers, to the alleged greed and laziness of those claiming benefits and the complacent largesse of a state which indiscriminately doles out welfare to meet their demands. This approach, a rhetorical and material triumph for the forces of neoliberalism, seeks to justify political attacks on the recipients of welfare by simultaneously subsuming them all into an underclass characterised as 'cheats', 'scroungers', 'workshy' and 'feckless', despite the fact that a majority of welfare recipients are in work and still struggling with lower wages, higher rents and increased costs of living.[5]

This remaking of the working class has been greatly assisted by a further inconsistency of the past twenty years: the fact that the insidious vanishing of direct articulations of social class within political and academic discourse has taken place alongside an upswing in media representations of working-class stereotypes. These depictions, almost invariably played for comic or grotesque effect, and equally overwhelmingly the creations of those hailing from a more privileged background than the characters they seek to portray, have proliferated over the past twenty years, with offerings from the films of Guy Richie to the novels of Martin Amis blighting the cultural landscape. In particular, the emergence within comedy and reality TV, as well as in the wider media, of the figure of the 'chav', has highlighted the continuation of class differences and antagonisms which go unacknowledged in official discourse.

'Chav' is a multivalent and unstable signifier, and has served many uses before settling into its present form. The strength of feeling with which many working-class people resent and refuse the idea of 'chav' as being synonymous with 'working-class' is too frequently glossed over in analyses of the 'chav' phenomenon. In one sense the modern use of 'chav' represents nothing more than the continued division, at least as old as industrialisation itself, of the poor into 'rough' and 'respectable' categories, with the former characterised by their absence of 'respectable' employment and their tendency towards the 'disre-spectable': excess drinking and drug taking, sexual licen-tiousness, petty crime, casual violence, brashness and vulgarity. 'Chav' has become a more or less nationally recognised term, but the stereotype it signifies is an agglomeration of several local variations of the term, all drawing on the rough/respectable division; its myriad of precursors include 'townie', 'ned', 'scally', and perhaps ultimately, 'common'. These expressions are used within communities to delineate internal hierarchies, based on an assumed connection between employment and respectability, rooted in a context where 'respectable' work was easier to obtain and its refusal more easily interpreted as irresponsible and dissolute. Part of Thatcherism's project involved the intensifying of such divisions – taking no account of the impact of an altered economic landscape – and, through policies such as the sale of council housing, the encouragement of a section of the working class to aspire to and identify with an individualist, 'respectable' middle-class lifestyle. While no one would deny that the term 'chav' is still used to indicate such gradations, these older and more familiar meanings are distinct from the current political use of 'chav', in which the word is used to section off an entire community by those at a socioeconomic remove from it. This argument is not about seeking a sympathetic view of real-world 'chavs', in all their infinite variety, but about the specific 'chav' stereotype as it has taken hold in popular culture, and the political uses made of it.

The early 70s panic over 'mugging' has been analysed as the politicised and media-legitimated reconfiguring of an established form of street crime into a threat to public order requiring immediate material intervention.[6] The 'chav', too, is an old and familiar antagonist reconstructed for political purposes. In *Chavs: The demonization of the working class*, Owen Jones went some way towards entrenching the word's meaning, at least in left and liberal analyses, as a derogatory term for the working class, used about that group rather than by them. When used in the sense Jones discusses, 'chav' tends to be stripped of any previous connotations and conflated with 'lower socioeconomic group', regardless of internal divisions or other forms of self-expression by individuals within that group. This reworking of the term has consolidated 'chav' as a media and political cipher, in which neutral signifiers are reconfigured as wholly negative in the manner described by Stanley Cohen in his work on 'folk devils and moral panics' which threaten the social order, both categories which also comfortably fit the 'chav'.[7] In this manner, the baseball cap which graces the cover of Jones's book, the 'Croydon facelift' achieved by a scraped-back high ponytail, the gold hoop earrings and the Burberry check, are taken to be emblematic of 'chav' culture and imbued with exclusively negative or comic associations, to the extent that the Burberry fashion label, disconcerted at its popularity among 'chav' figures, was moved to 'fight back' by disassociating itself.

The 'chav' stereotypes which have gained media prominence and cultural currency are those which are politically useful, being amenable to adoption for narratives which draw on the idea of a scrounging and feckless underclass to justify political attacks on all of us lower down the socioeconomic scale. Cuts to housing or child benefit, for instance, impact on many working families, but the issue tends to be presented as targeted at an undeserving (and highly unrepresentative) 'chav' demographic – in this case usually a woman who 'churns out' children with no intention of supporting them through marriage or employment. The extent to which 'chav' has become associated in the popular imagination with the working class as a whole, rather than an internally identified, lumpen subset of it, is demonstrated by the ability of *Times* journalist Peter Watson to refer to Martin Amis' 2012 novel *Lionel Asbo*, a clunky riff on the lives of a lazily imagined underclass, as a 'lampoon' not of 'chavs' but of 'proletarian culture', going on to specify this culture as one of 'moronic brutality and vapidity' and 'frightening ignorance', ignoring the equally frightening ignorance implied by the elision of class gradations to this degree.[8]

Official discourse regards the working class with a peculiar blend of contempt and sentimentality. The white working-class male, when behaving in a government- and media-approved 'respectable' manner, is upheld as a dying breed, the noble epitome of an indigenous British culture supposedly under threat from immigration, feminism, socialism, the European Court of Human Rights and its outriders political correctness and health and safety; a minority besieged in his own land. He has no female equivalent, only a wifely accessory, whose unpaid domestic and reproductive labour must necessarily orbit his respectable paid employment. This kind of prelapsarian idyll, now supposedly fragmented by the female-friendly forces of progressive modernity, underlies both Willetts' conceit of the working-class male displaced from education and employment by the forward march of women, and Glasman's conceit of the hectored, long-suffering husband of an inconveniently educated and empowered wife. Again, in both these pictures working-class women are conspicuous by their absence. But, in this external construction of working-class identity, the 'chav' is this character's contemptible foil, the undeservingly thriving villain to his respectably, contentedly poor hero: unsympathetic, disruptive, unruly, insouciant, contemptuous of authority rather than deferential to it – and, very often, female.

The demonisation of the female
working class

As stereotypes go, 'chav' is remarkably even-handed: for every lager-swilling lout invoked by panicky editorials, there's a single mother, for every Wayne Rooney a Waynetta Slob. 'Chav' signifiers, in fact, make it possible to de-emphasise or efface one's femininity with gender-neutral baseball caps, shapeless leisurewear and scraped-back hair. But the female 'chav' is nevertheless a recognisable figure and a heavily classed and sexualised one, portrayals of which involve images of deprivation and dysfunction (pram-pushing and pregnant teenage girls, slovenly and self-absorbed single mothers) rather than, say, the targets of 'chavertising', an early-2000s marketing strategy which defined 'chavs' as an upwardly-mobile subculture with spending power, whose members prioritised consumption and conspicuous displays of wealth. Many of these former images, significantly, are self-conscious or pastiche portrayals by those not identifying as a permanent part of the subculture: a kind of chav-drag. The prime example of this is of course *Little Britain*'s Vicky Pollard, one of the oddest fictional stereotypes to be fixed as a moral standard since the elder George Bush instructed Americans to be more like the Waltons and less like the Simpsons. The uses made in political and media discourse of the figure of the female 'chav' are a vivid illustration of the process by which abstract meanings are articulated through female figures, and analysing the types of women stereotyped as 'chavs' exposes the particularly virulent strain of misogyny which 'chav'-hatred can contain. As Owen Jones has also noted, this tendency reached a somewhat hysterical pitch in a 2006 rant by *soi-disant* libertarian conservative James Delingpole, in which Pollard is made to embody:

several of the great scourges of contemporary Britain: aggressive female gangs of embittered, hormonal, drunken teenagers; gym-slip mums who choose to get pregnant as a career option; pasty-faced, lard-gutted slappers who'll drop their knickers in the blink of an eye...[9]

Typically, as here, an anti-'chav' stance cloaks a thoroughly unpleasant perpetuation of damaging stereotypes of working-class women (sexual promiscuity, sexual precociousness, a thoughtless or scheming lack of protection resulting in pregnancy) as well as a proscribing of non-traditional behaviour (women existing outside traditional family roles, deriving financial support from the state rather than a husband). Anti-'chav' commentators reveal a disquieting obsession with the presumed licentiousness and promiscuity of working-class women, whose irresponsibility, aggressive lack of deference, and refusal of traditional family and community hierarchies, must be politically penalised. Meanwhile, government rhetoric insistently plays on the stereotype of the idle and recklessly promiscuous single mother, along with the moral decline, sexual depravity, and social disintegration she is held to represent, to validate the wider reduction or removal of state support from benefits claimants.[10] All this with barely a glance at context or circumstance, with the working-class 'bad girl' understood not in terms of poverty or social exclusion but in neoliberal terms of individual moral degeneracy, and the inadequacies of single mothers viewed as purely individual failings or pathology rather than related to their demoralising lack of adequate financial and material resources.[11] This is of a piece with the reconfiguring of poor families and communities as 'problem families' or 'antisocial' elements, in reports and studies which pay little attention to the problems caused to individuals and collectives by the economic and political vagaries and failings of the past thirty years. It also, as Beverley Skeggs has observed, continues the historical representation of working-class women via their 'deviant' sexuality, rather than the possibilities for 'rebellion, heroism and authenticity' which the working-class identity has historically held for men.[12]

The right in Britain, which traditionally spends less energy than the left on debating semantics, has wasted little time in elevating the 'chav' into an avatar for the irresponsible, idle and undeserving poor. In 2009, Patrick Flynn in the *Daily Express* marshalled popular cultural representations of a reckless and feckless underclass in the interests of reviving rhetoric from an age when the Tories were happy to openly play 'the nasty party':

> *After Peter Lilley told the 1992 Tory conference, in a parody of The Mikado: 'I've got a little list of benefit offenders who I'll soon be rooting out and who never would be missed', he was condemned as nasty and uncaring. How many would take issue with him now, I wonder?... Popular culture, which once endorsed the liberal view that Lilley was a bigot, has now accepted the reality of the situation he outlined all those years ago. The irresponsibility of the underclass has become a television staple, from the Jeremy Kyle show to dramas like Shameless and documentaries from the meanest streets....*[13]

Lilley's 'benefit offenders' included, inevitably, 'young ladies who get pregnant just to jump the housing queue'. Since taking office in 2010, the Coalition has overseen an intensification of Lilleyesque language in politics and the media, with much of popular culture now uncritically reflecting or actively supporting such rhetoric rather than examining or challenging it. At any given moment, the dominant class and gender representations in popular culture may be related to contemporary political imperatives, showing their audience how and how not to behave, reflecting dominant values, concerns and anxieties, providing aspirational images or dreadful warnings. The gendered, racially anxious, and class-based disgust evident in anti-'chav' rhetoric has played a defining role in this, as part of a disconcerting trend in popular culture towards punching downwards through mocking and appropriative representations. The proliferation of 'chav' stereotypes has taken place alongside a narrowing of access to the arts and entertainment world, which has meant that much contemporary comedy, film and television, as well as music, is now produced by those whose experience and understanding of backgrounds different to their own is limited. Apart from Kathy Burke as the proto-'chav' Waynetta Slob, the only relatively non-privileged mainstream comedian to draw on this stereotype has been Catherine Tate as Lauren Cooper, a character who, compared to Pollard, is nuanced and sympathetic (Cooper's 2007 Comic Relief appearance, for instance, has as its pay-off her unsuspected and incongruous knowledge of Shakespeare, rather than a further display of the depths of her blissful ignorance). The political crisis of working-class representation is also a cultural one, and the two are interlinked: labelling, shaming and ridiculing the working class through the use of signifiers and stereotypes in popular culture is a means of making the political, social and economic clampdown occasioned by austerity appear less harsh than it is, while the restriction of working-class access to the conduits of mainstream popular culture also limits the ability to strike back.

After I presented a version of this argument on the feminist website *Bad Reputation*, suggesting 'chav' as an intersection of sexism and classism, an example of such thinking in action was identified by Ciara O'Connor in an analysis of public responses to the appearance of a 'sex tape' featuring N-Dubz vocalist Tulisa Contostavlos. O'Connor points out:

> *The word 'chav' ... loaded with class prejudice, was ubiquitous in*

tweets on the subject ... the words 'slut' and 'chav' were used pretty much interchangeably. Tweet after tweet focused obsessively on Tulisa's working class background: her 'chavvery'. Many expressed a lack of surprise at the tape, because they 'always knew she was a chav, was just a matter of time really before she made one'.[14]

The female 'chav' fits into narratives of slut-shaming and taste-policing, implying unladylike promiscuity, lack of restraint, and vulgarity in dress, speech and behaviour. All heavily classed presentations, these are held to be especially objectionable when observed in women, with sexual excess seen as a central signifier of 'disrespectable' femininity. Intersections like this make explicit several implications of the discourse around the figure of the female 'chav', not least the conflation of sexuality and class to invoke the Victorian and Edwardian spectre of working-class women, with their hazardous lack of morality, taste and discrimination and their unregulated, untrammelled sexuality, spawning hundreds of equally depraved and financially burdensome children. What it also does, however, is to again reveal the way in which 'chav' can function as an intra-class line dividing the respectable from the rough. Many of those attacking Contostavlos as a 'chav' were women who might themselves be labelled as 'chavs' by those of a higher socioeconomic bracket, concerned to distinguish themselves in turn from women they perceived as less respectable. 'Respectability', in this case, is measured by sexual standards, as it might elsewhere be by behavioural standards or style of dress, and these class-inflected ideas of 'respectability' can function as a means of restricting women's sexual agency as well as a tactic of divide-and-rule. The fact that these internal differences, articulated by the working class itself, tend to be ignored by a media intent on lumping together all representatives of a particular demographic under the 'chav' banner, and treating them accordingly with prurience, pity or contempt, reveals the misuse of 'chav' in much contemporary discourse. Moreover, it highlights the term's usefulness to a political class intent on demonising a whole sector of the population, regardless of that population's deeply felt and strongly voiced resistance to the identity.

'Chav' is (not just) a feminist issue

Just as, across the UK, there are people who call themselves working-class despite the erosion of that identity in media and political discourse, so conversely there are working-class women who live and think according to feminist principles, but would be sceptical of or hostile to the idea of calling themselves feminists. In a salutary article in March 2012, working-class journalist Pavan Amara found that a variety of UK women viewed feminism as dominated by women of a more privileged background.[15] Often their alienation from mainstream feminism resulted from an absence of suitable entry points, notably access to higher education and the time and inclination to read books, blogs or broadsheets. However, the scepticism, indifference or hostility towards feminism expressed by Amara's interviewees was also generated by the impression of class-based exclusion, with one interviewee comparing it to a political party 'you know don't care about you anyway', demonstrating that the current widespread disenchantment with parliamentary politics extends for many to a feeling of indiscriminate, absolutist disenfranchisement with activist groups and representative structures.

A number of feminists on- and offline have made welcome attempts to integrate class into their analyses, and of course socialist feminism and much of the revolutionary left engage positively with feminism as an expression of class struggle. Valuable work has been done to analyse the gendered impact of the post-2008 economic crisis and the subsequent imposition of austerity, from the job losses and spread of precarity suffered by employment sectors in which women are disproportionately represented, to cuts in childcare services and women's refuges.[16] In mainstream politics and media, however, there remains a tendency for working-class women themselves to appear in feminist discourse as objects to be seen rather than heard, expected to rely on middle-class activists to articulate demands on their behalf but considered too inarticulate or otherwise 'rough' to be directly engaged with. In May 2011 Baroness Hussein-Ece, Liberal Democrat peer and member of the Coalition's Commission for Equality and Human Rights, expressed herself on Twitter thus: '*Help. Trapped in a queue in chav-land. Woman behind me explaining latest EastEnders plot to mate, while eating largest bun I've ever seen*'. The consequent furore over this anaemic but indicative snippet of snobbery, issuing from a government appointee on matters of equality, illustrated the capacity for 'chav' to cause class-inflected cracks in the rhetoric and reality of egalitarianism. Social barriers to inter-class interaction within feminism are exacerbated by the fact that mainstream liberal feminism often foregrounds an academic and theoretical focus which, though valuable, is remote from practical considerations of material inequality, with the result that feminist analysis can seem off-puttingly abstract, irrelevant, and attuned only to middle-class concerns.

The claim that working-class women are excluded from feminism must of course be qualified. The idea of an absolute dichotomy between 'high theory' middle-class feminist activists and disenfranchised, politically unconscious working-class women demonstrates one of many pitfalls of insisting upon 'authentic' class identities. The 'chav', crucially, is represented as uneducated and often actively hostile to the idea of education, negating the possibility of self-improvement. But the idea that there are no grey areas, no available identities, between the volubly ignorant Vicky Pollard and an empowered and educated middle-class feminist leads to the double-bind whereby political engagement and consciousness raising is seen as automatically conferring class privilege and upward mobility upon an individual, thereby barring them from identifying with or being categorised as 'working-class'. Not only do many university-educated feminists come from working-class backgrounds, but working-class feminists form part of the long line of working-class autodidacts whose attraction to ideologies of emancipation partly results from the desire to articulate and analyse their own experiences. Indeed, part of the problem with 'chav' is that the label and stereotype obscure the past and present existence of this tradition. As with many types of activism, however, higher socioeconomic status undoubtedly increases the capacity of women to 'do' feminism, whether this stems from their increased likelihood of a university background, or their ability to afford help with living costs, childcare and housework, and hence to allocate more resources to activism, volunteering, conference-going, analysing current affairs, and even producing blog content.

If the class-inflected experience of feminism's mainstream proponents influence what 'the movement' presents as priorities, so does a mainstream media attuned to the sensationalist and the shallowly sexy. Pop-cultural presentations can and do misrepresent feminism as much as class, and the mainstream emphasis on a class-inflected variety of feminism, preoccupied either with abstract theory or remote 'lifestyle' concerns, does little to engage with the material inequality increasingly experienced by a majority of women or to draw meaningfully on the traditions of working-class feminism. Working-class women's exclusion from mainstream feminism, despite the condescension and class essentialism implicit in some of its manifestations, remains a valid critique which has yet to be addressed. Acknowledging that the discourse around 'chavs' can be disingenuous, and can provide a cover for denigrating the social agency and sexual autonomy of working-class women, as well as for wider political attacks on the unemployed and working poor, would significantly enrich mainstream feminism and challenge the perception of it as irrelevant outside an academic and metropolitan elite.

Recognition and confronting of the 'chav' stereotype as a method of class demonisation, while both welcome and long overdue, has not only paid insufficient attention to the gendered dimensions of the term but also sought unhelpfully to redress the idea of 'chav' by proposing equally inadequate and exclusionary models of working-class identity. Several critiques of 'chav' in both the conservative and liberal media have advanced other, supposedly more positive, working-class identities which draw heavily on the figure of the noble and oppressed worker – invariably white and male – while others have centred on the idea of defending 'the white working class' as a neglected ethnic group on whom 'chav' is a slur. This, with obvious dubiousness, posits the 'authentic' working class as white and masculine. Within these parameters, the 'chav' appears as both a modernised version of Marx's lumpenproletariat, implicitly feminised by dint of the inability to express a securely masculine identity based on being a 'respectably' employed breadwinner, and a figure of 'borderline whiteness' invoked in what Imogen Tyler identifies as 'an attempt to differentiate between respectable and non-respectable forms of whiteness'.[17] While there is plainly a need for the left to engage with working-class disenfranchisement and *ressentiment*, rather than abandoning the field to right-wing analyses, white and masculinist working-class particularism not only risks intensifying intra-class antipathies based on race, sexuality and gender, but also undermines the idea of the working class as a category based on an underlying commonality of interest between diverse intersectional groups. Exclusionary constructions of working-class identity ignore, for instance, the historical involvement of women in constitutional and extraparliamentary movements for social, economic and labour reform; that the question of women's suffrage was presented to Parliament in 1832 as part of the general struggle for reform and extension of the franchise to non-property-holding and working men; and the solidarity provided during the 1984–5 miners' strike by both the LGBT community and the organised support of miners' wives. They ignore, too, that deindustrialisation, structural unemployment, and loss of skilled work, which has destroyed a former source of masculine status and self-respect, has also weakened what could be a source of empowerment and consciousness-raising for women. The factory as a potential hub of female working-class solidarity, an unfashionable species of feminism lately commodified in the 2010 film *Made in Dagenham*, was testified to by another of Pavan Amara's interviewees:

When I was a child the unions were strong, my mother was a working-class woman and she related to feminism in a practical way. She didn't need the right words, or to be well-versed. She saw it as female workers standing up to the male bosses who owned the factory. Now, unions are weaker and feminism has become increasingly academic, meaning you have to be educated to be taken seriously. Put that together and you'll get a lot of working-class females out there who feel they have no voice.

Recuperating these traditions, and these models of male and female empowerment, is plainly inconceivable while in the grip of mass unemployment, recession and austerity. Strategies for remedying this situation will require the left to take the initiative in integrating and consolidating critiques of neoliberalism based on race and gender as well as class, in order to realise the political agency of a currently ostracised, ridiculed and demonised demographic. As part of this, refusal and challenging of the 'chav' stereotype should be done in terms which recognise the diverse and intersectional nature of working-class identities for both men and women.

PART TWO:

WORKING FOR THE CLAMPDOWN: CLASS AND GENDER IN BRITPOP AND AFTER

2.1 The Day after the Revolution

'As soon as people realise that the majority of people in this country take drugs, then the better off we'll all be.'
– Noel Gallagher (Oasis), 1997

Looking back at 90s Britain, we are used to seeing in colour. In particular, what stands out is the red white and blue of the union flag: Cool Britannia, the reanimated corpse of Swinging London. Red, white, and blue covering up the loutishly louche Liam Gallagher on the cover of *Vanity Fair*, straining with iconic splendour around Geri Halliwell at the 1997 Brit awards, or fluttering in the hands of ecstatic acolytes for Blair's victory ride into Downing Street. Viewed through other filters, however, the 90s were several shades of grey, limp and listless, stewed in pre-millennial tension. While Blairism's Technicolor iconography may have anchored itself in memories of the 90s, the seven lean years preceding it are perhaps more fundamental in understanding the decade. As the 90s began, history had apparently ended, and accordingly the country appeared to be stagnating from the top down: the 1992 election saw Labour under Kinnock snatch an excruciating defeat from the jaws of victory, ushering in a period of stultifying political malaise. Over the next five years the initially triumphalist government of John Major, mired in a mudslide of hypocrisy, arrogance, incompetence and corruption, took a painfully long time to die. As political horrors went, after the scorched-earth approach of Thatcherism this felt bland and mundane, a salting of the earth with a million little grains of injustice, stupidity and sadly comic indignity. Testing the bounds of credibility and tolerance, on and on the administration shambled, shedding MPs and integrity by what seemed like the day, bumblingly overseeing a scabbing over of 80s-inflicted wounds – railway privatisation, benefit cuts, the

Criminal Justice Act – until at times it genuinely seemed as if there was no end in sight, that this was a government impossible to indict and that all the future held was the prospect of a grey cricket shoe stamping on a human face forever.

One interpretation of the media-managed outpouring of grief which followed the death of Diana, Princess of Wales, in September 1997, was that its sudden and shocking nature, received as a barely credible rupture in what had seemed a life of bulletproof privilege, had given the nation a much-needed emotional pressure-valve. Focusing less on Diana's position of lifelong advantage and more on her hidden unhappiness, her charity work, and her Oprahfied soul-baring, offered the chance to cathartically contrast such misery-fuelled empathy and altruism with the individualist selfishness and greed which the 80s had elevated as social and economic driving-forces. Finally recognising the divisive changes the country had undergone and the damage incurred, so the theory ran, 'we' were mourning what 'we' had become. Diana-hysteria, though, was less the catalyst for this than the channel through which it most publicly erupted. The 90s, especially the years surrounding the ascension of Anthony Charles Lynton Blair, were suffused with the idea of post-traumatic healing, regrouping, and renewal, in sheepish recognition of the fallout from the conflicts and divisions of the Tory years – but with both culpability and redress framed in terms that were emphatically emotional rather than economic.[18]

Instrumental in this was New Labour's attempt, in tandem with its own post-socialist rebranding, to conjure a vision of the country as diverse, permissive and culturally dynamic. This rebranding would embrace the cultural and sexual revolution where Thatcher and Major had deplored it, and define Britain's place in the world not through the imperial past, or indeed through manufacturing, but through the burgeoning music, art, film and fashion of 'Cool Britannia', our shiny new motor of national renewal and economic growth. Cool Britannia's cultural artefacts were useful for both economy and hegemony: in the wake of Britain's declining global influence, and the incipient decentralisation of power via Scottish and Welsh devolution, anxieties over national identity might be soothed by a nostalgic construction of smart, creative and self-assured post-imperial Britishness, channelling potential restlessness or discontent into the urge to contentedly celebrate, consume, and accept. The country's hope now lay in ideas, designs, and brands which could project an image of 'New Britain', even if these projections were ironically fuelled by hagiographical invoking of the old, whether the glories of 60s guitar pop or England's victory in the 1966 World Cup.

This branding exercise was manifestly superficial, a red, white and blue sticking-plaster over a gaping wound in the body economic. New Labour's acceptance of the neoliberal settlement – the alleged end of history, ideology, and any alternative to Thatcherite economics – restricted their scope for material improvement, particularly in post-industrial regions devastated by the 80s. Under Major, a second round of pit closures and the long, sad hold-out of the Liverpool dockers had planted a conclusive boot on the coffin-lid of industrial organisation and industry itself, and New Labour in opposition had concentrated less upon the unsexy struggles of an apparently doomed demographic and more on the promise to deliver such communities, slumped and comatose, into the embrace of a tamed free market. In government, the handwringing reports produced by John Prescott's coalfield task force on post-industrial areas of Britain, with their inhabitants' 'unique combination' of concentrated joblessness, physical isolation, poor infrastructure and severe physical and mental health problems, prompted only a renewed emphasis on attracting employment – any employment – as short-term, panicked panacea. Flimsy sticking-plaster sectors – call centres, fast food outlets, cardboard-box factories – grew like bindweed, with little or no attention paid to the psychological aftermath of economic trauma: the spread of mental illness, petty crime, addiction and dependency. These criteria would of course be prominent a decade later in the condemning of such areas as full of undeserving 'chavs', more securely consigning them to the scrapheap. In the 80s, this other Britain might have had some clout, some class, but in the 90s we were frankly an embarrassment, out of place and out of time, and for all the recognition we were granted in Cool Britannia's pantheon we may as well have vanished down a disused mineshaft.

The Britpop narrative is by now familiar: Suede in 1993 made their initial feints at a glamorously grubby alternative to British indie's meandering present and the transatlantic supremacy of grunge; following this, Blur's slicker and quicker musical dilettantism settled into a cohesive brand of Anglocentric guitar pop with *Modern Life is Rubbish*; indie's advance upon the mainstream accelerated in 1994 with the release of Blur's *Parklife* (an album, like its predecessor, showcasing several broad-brush working-class taxonomies), before going supernova that same year with Oasis' *Definitely Maybe*. There followed a Camden-centric rush of bands straining to fit or unwillingly squeezed into the newly-set 'Britpop' mould, along with the appearance by rock star *manqué* and newly elected Labour leader Tony Blair at the 1994 *Q* magazine awards. The spring of 1995 saw Blair and various associates taking tea with both Albarn and Oasis manager Alan McGee, followed by that summer's 'Battle of Britpop', in which Blur and Oasis faced off in an NME-manufactured scrap for the top spot. With both musicians and a highly politicised music press reflecting popular revulsion at a Conservative regime awash with sleaze and incompetence, Blair's intervention at the 1996 Brit Awards, with a speech saluting bands of his youth including the Beatles and the Kinks, seemed only natural. Blair's relative youth and platform of modernisation also facilitated his creep towards Britpop, a movement which appeared to chime with New Labour's forging, in both senses, of a prospective young, cool and prosperous national future. For its 1997 campaign song, New Labour adopted D:Ream's Things Can Only Get Better, a song first released four years previously when its vapid euphoria could only have been seen in political terms as a bad joke, but as the fanfare for a new governmental dawn it seemed entirely appropriate.

It remains difficult to bury Britpop without praising it. After British indie's submergence in the nebulous wastes of shoegaze and baggy, the relief provided by the emergence of directional, ebullient music, made by the unabashedly ambitious, slotted neatly into New Labour's promotion of the 90s as confident and fresh, conjuring a giddy metropolitan optimism assisted by an economic boom which was only decisively ended with the banking crisis of 2008. In the grey Majorite 90s, much of indie had drawn on punk's reaction to a similarly stultifying and visibly diminished idea of England, and on post-punk's creation of insular subcultural alternatives to an inhospitable or indifferent mainstream. Both of these emphasised the virtues of independence over acceptance of commercial imperatives. The rising popularity and hype of Britpop, however, with its celebratory contentedness and accommodation of mainstream values, was accompanied by galloping commercialisation as Camden churned out ever more skinny, pale, floppy-fringed and formulaic adherents to the Britpop blueprint. As Blur, Oasis and their imitators became guaranteed money-spinners, and the manufactured rivalry between both bands in summer 1995 entrenched the idea of the number one single as the *ne plus ultra* of musical achievement, the mass market increasingly edged out the margins as an arena of interest, with experimentalism and eccentricity compromised in the pursuit of chart success. Desire for a high chart placing need not, of course, be a bad thing, just as holding fast to an ideal of subcultural purity does not automatically equate to musical quality. The Manic Street Preachers, during their early chafing against their initial indie confines, were vocally unresistant to the lure of selling a million; in 1991, their tongue-in-cheek manifesto was 'release one album that will outsell *Appetite for Destruction*, tour the world, headline Wembley for three nights and then burn out'. But what the Manics offered was in radical, not to say comical, conflict with their desires: at the time of this pronouncement, their selling a million records would have involved the commercial and popular acceptance of their frequently preposterous musical blend of Guns N' Roses and McCarthy and their sub-Situationist lyrics and aesthetic. Their mock commercial vision involved implausibly far-reaching upheaval rather than slavish adherence to existing convention. Kenickie, one of the 90s' least deservedly forgotten groups, also 'wanted hits, not obscurity', but not at the expense of their self-expression. By contrast, the post-Oasis rush for outfits cut from the same lucrative cloth saw bands and record companies, including indie labels, increasingly go for tried and tested templates over ripping up the map, flooding the market with models of diminishing return, interest and functionality.

Cool Britannia, like much of 90s culture and politics, appears in retrospect as a flight of white-powder-fuelled fancy, built on empty buzzwords which belied material reality, and entrenching an emphasis on commercial success to which was sacrificed genuine experimentalism, innovation and long-term growth. It seems significant that Britpop proper appeared to evaporate at the moment of Blairism's triumph. The Oasis/Blur pseudo-contest of 1995 can be seen as, among other things, a foreshadowing of New Labour's electoral victory: an overhyped and profit-driven illusion of choice between two versions of an overriding trend, with the new boss substantially the same as the old boss. As New Labour took office, the bullish assurance of its pop-cultural favourites had already begun to recede:

Blur's self-titled release that year saw them rehabilitate, of all things, the US lo-fi guitar music they had formerly disparaged, while Oasis stuck to their established formula for the avidly anticipated *Be Here Now*, but turned in a dated-on-arrival, cocaine-bloated and overproduced disappointment. Britpop, having by now marginalised or stifled the eclectic alternatives which had previously flourished in British indie, left us with a post-Oasis rump of guitar bands under the banner of 'lad rock' (or Dadrock, or Noelrock, labels all equally indicative), defined by unambitious hedonism and stagnant nostalgia. Britpop's affair with Blair, like Britpop itself, was very quickly all over bar the shouting. John Prescott's attendance at the 1998 Brits saw an ice-bucket upended over him by veteran anarchist band Chumbawamba, who had experienced unlikely chart success with the paean to resilience Tubthumping; Damon Albarn declared himself 'disgusted' with the government's education policies; the *NME* put Blair on its cover with the strapline 'Ever get the feeling you've been cheated?'; and suspicions about the individualist arrogance at the heart of the New Labour project were scathingly articulated in Pulp's Cocaine Socialism. The Britpop party was messily winding down, its momentum lost, its attendees whimpering and withdrawn, and, as the sun came up on a supposedly new, emotionally rescued Britain, the lamps were going out all over Camden.

2.2 90s

Death of a party

'That's the extraordinary thing about the 90s - we feel separate from the rest of existence. We feel as though we know everything that's gone before and we use it all and, therefore, none of us feels real. There's never, ever before been such a pre-occupation with defining whether people are real or not. But I hope we're getting out of that a bit now. I think everyone just wants to be a bit more naive about it all, there's a lot less self-examination going on.'
– Damon Albarn (Blur), 1995

Suede's 1993 debut, claustrophobic with council flats, concrete, and lasciviously grimy guitars, was lauded along with Blur's more pointed and pantomime *Modern Life is Rubbish* for establishing the quotidian detail of British lives as worthy of commentary, however mannered or caricatured. But early 90s Britain had life outside Camden, and already had music which engaged with and reflected contemporary concerns and anxieties rather than attempting to mould a self-consciously atavistic 'British' identity. Much of this music was explicitly politicised and informed by a broader oppositional impulse rooted in 70s and 80s subculture, from the Manic Street Preachers' early scattergun Situationism to the threads of trance and techno which ran through countercultural tributaries including the free festival scene, Reclaim the Streets and the nascent anti-globalisation movement. The 90s music press, too, gave a platform to anti-racist and anti-war activism, treating its subject as part of a wider oppositional culture in which an angry and intelligent political consciousness was considered an asset rather than an embarrassment. More sophisticated than the sledgehammer sludge of many more overtly political publications, a certain left-wing sensibility shone through the best of

90s music writing like sunlight through stained glass. The degree to which a coherent politicised subculture revolved around music, in a way currently unthinkable, can be measured by the political response to it. The 1994 Criminal Justice Bill proposed an increase in police powers, significantly reduced the right of suspects to silence, and criminalised previously civil offences including hunt sabotage and anti-road protesting. It also, notoriously, sought to outlaw gatherings where music characterised by 'repetitive beats' might be played. Drafted in an atmosphere of twitchy moral panic, this explicit legislative swipe at rave, house and techno galvanised some of the least political of my peer group and drew an unsurprisingly hostile response from bands themselves: Dreadzone's Chomsky-sampling Fight The Power advocated active resistance to the bill while the sleevenotes for The Prodigy's *Music for the Jilted Generation* offered the critique. 'How can the government stop young people having a good time? Fight this bollocks'.

As an example of the simmering discontent simplistically but soundly expressed in much early-90s music, take (I Want to) Kill Somebody, the enduring legacy of a power-punk trio from Welwyn Garden City called S*M*A*S*H. They were part of the movement styled New Wave of New Wave, one of several which Britpop left steamrollered in its wake, and which looked back in form and content to restlessly disgruntled agit-punk and post-punk. More often a lumpen pub-rock trudge than the spiky speedfreak rush to which they aspired, S*M*A*S*H nevertheless had one song that shone diamond-like in the seemingly infinite slurry of the Major years. In the summer of 1994, (I Want to) Kill Somebody sounded simultaneously like the best and the worst thing I'd ever heard. Its lyrics included a hitlist consisting of the Tory front bench, reeled off in vocals choking on the leash, and its video apparently showed the band's bassist biting off the Prime Minister's penis. Available in record shops for a single day, and inevitably banned on most radio stations, the song nevertheless scraped into the Top Forty, where, over Sunday tea in living-rooms across the land, it snapped and snarled behind heavily censoring bars of silence, a ludicrous and perfect proposition. Clattering and squealing, piling sixth-form radical posturing on back-from-the-pub bluster, achingly well-intentioned and uncushioned by a spare ounce of sophistication, the song was exactly what 1994 deserved. Like the anti-government, anti-war and anti-aristocracy handbills and prints produced in the wave of English popular radicalism which followed the French Revolution, (I Want to) Kill Somebody was lurid, rudimentary and cartoonishly violent, unburdened by any developed analysis but driven by a basic materialist outrage at patently absurd injustice. This vulgarity of opposition was an appropriate and necessary response to a state similarly lacking in nuance, understanding or analysis; the government in question was, after all, sufficiently arrogant, out of touch, paranoid and staggeringly thick to think that it could and should attempt to regulate the number of beats to which one could publicly dance.

In addition to grunge, hip-hop, rave, ragga, gabba, jungle, trip-hop, post-rock, R&B and dancehall, elements of all of which found a home in the 90s charts, a large amount of pre-Britpop music took its cue from influences outside the tradition of white British guitar-rock, whether Saint Etienne's nods to 60s soul and French pop; Stereolab's overtly communist indietronica; the trip-hop triumvirate of Tricky, Portishead and Massive Attack; Cornershop's ramshackle fusions or the sampling-infused post-punk of Disco Inferno. Dance notably remained in the ascendency throughout the decade, with names like the Prodigy, the Chemical Brothers and Fatboy Slim as ubiquitous as those of Oasis and Blur. Plenty of music outside the Britpop pale felt identifiably British and reliably reflected 90s Britain, even if doing so was not a major preoccupation of the bands concerned. The insistence on defining a narrow national identity in the early 90s had in fact been largely the preserve of the right. In 1993, Major had co-opted Orwell's sardonic depiction of 'old maids bicycling to holy communion through the morning mist' into a bloody-mindedly nostalgic vision of Britain which also encompassed cricket, beer and 'invincible green suburbs', while the temporary electoral success of the British National Party in parts of East London involved the contestation of 'Britishness' as part of their disingenuous and opportunistic exploitation of the areas' economic and political neglect. Pre-Britpop music contained elements which sought to combat this on a broad front, arguing for a culturally eclectic and diverse Britain whose roots were deeper than the Blairite branding exercise that Britpop became. Pre-Britpop and even early Britpop bands tended to engage with the country as they found it, rather than fixating on a normative ideal of national identity which became in its own way as sentimental and exclusionary a confection as Major's.

As revealed by Cool Britannia's momentary bolt-ons, 'cool Cymru' and 'cool Caledonia', Britishness is a nebulous and insincere concept at best. The former pseudo-movement, an awkward agglomeration of the Manic Street Preachers' sudden success and the coincidental surge in Welsh bands of varying quality and longevity, was mentioned in the House of Commons as marking a 'new wave of confidence in the Welsh nation', which in itself went some way towards complicating the notion of 'Britannia'. 1994, the year Britpop broke with *Parklife* and *Definitely Maybe*, was also the year of Suede's consciously anti-Britpop *Dog Man Star* and the Manic Street Preachers' *The Holy Bible*, an album antithetical in style and subject matter to the year's Britpop canon, and which formed a nexus of alternative arguments and concerns. Absent from, or actively refusing, many of the narratives of its time, especially the twin triumphalisms of Britpop and Blairism, *The Holy Bible* stubbornly retained other narratives of which its era was characterised by the shedding and suppression (the impact of the end of the cold war, the 90s confessional turn, the 'crisis of masculinity' and other socio-political peculiarities stemming from having grown up in Thatcher-damaged, post-industrial parts of the country) and, in its angst, anxiety, rage and self-loathing, the album vividly expressed the tensions which boiled between these two Britains.

There was more interesting and more representative material than Britpop, then, but there was little so politically expedient. From one perspective, Britpop was New Wave of New Wave smugly scrubbed-up and shorn of its more interesting edges, including its politics. For aspirant rock stars from the mid-90s onwards, with the continuing Tory onslaught on Labour's core constituency going largely unchallenged ideologically by the Labour leadership, and Blair courting the Britpop glitterati, being angry wasn't a good look. The bands clustered around the Cool Britannia banner couched their social critique in mockery or condescension, their audience kept at a breezily cool arm's length rather than yanked in for S*M*A*S*H's breathlessly urgent close-up. A depoliticised wilful optimism won out over the trenchantly bleak perspective of bands like Blaggers ITA, whose 1991 effort *Fuck Fascism, Fuck Capitalism, Society's Fucked* is perhaps the best lairily succinct summation of a certain late twentieth-century mindset we're likely to get. As Britpop became profitably institutionalised, suddenly everything was permitted – sexism, chauvinism, xenophobia and ignorance – on the understanding that it was ironic. Meaning it, leaving yourself open to face-value criticism for views genuinely advocated or principles sincerely held, became about as publicly admissible as voting Tory.

Stereotypes: there must be more to life

'...there's no point in being a willing passenger and then trying to draw the line. It's such a classic middle-class thing to have a good time and then look in the mirror and you don't recognise yourself. Well, I'm sorry but I didn't look in the mirror and there wasn't a time I didn't recognise myself. I just got pissed.'
– James Dean Bradfield (Manic Street Preachers), 1994

As Britpop's tentacles uncoiled, extending from Camden into the wider world of New Labour, New Britain, it grew increasingly unreconstructed and exclusionary. Iconic Britpop tended to involve the unexamined articulation of class representations which foregrounded whiteness and maleness, ignoring the huge variations in experience and presentation of class in favour of positioning mawkish, broad-brush and condescending stereotypes on a queasily ironic axis of satire and self-aggrandisement. In this, it reflected and reinforced a wider cultural turn which gleefully rejected the perceived stifling excesses of 80s 'political correctness' in favour of the hollow postfeminist triumphalism of 'girl power' on one hand, and, on the other, 'new laddism'. New laddism was a downwardly-aspirational approximation of masculinity, constructed in opposition to the self-consciously liberal and sexually hesitant 'new man' of the 80s, and based around the consumption of lager, football, soft porn and the championing of all three in the new breed of men's magazines kick-started in 1994 by *Loaded*. Football in particular, after a decade of class-inflected anxieties over hooliganism and dehumanising emphasis on crowd control by the government, media and police had eventuated in the deaths of 96 people at Hillsborough in 1989, was reconfigured as part of a gentrified lifestyle choice for the professional classes. The proliferation of downwardly-aspirational signifiers stripped of meaning extended through art, film, music, media and politics, and this appropriation of working-class identifiers provided cover for an affectation of attitudes which were consciously, 'knowingly', pre-feminist, chauvinist and anti-intellectual.[19]

In the course of this, women artists tended to be squeezed to the margins, and their media presentation restricted, by the elevation of 'lad bands', the testosterone-heavy dominance (with some honourable and dishonourable exceptions) of the music press and men's magazines, and the focus on male key players and kingmakers, from Anderson, Albarn and the Gallaghers to Alan McGee. As will be discussed more fully below, 90s indie harboured several largely forgotten identities which diverged both from the vacant consumerism of girl-power and from new laddism's deferent camp follower, the 'ladette'. Besides Elastica, Shampoo and Kenickie, there was the impeccably Brightonian queer feminism of Echobelly's Sonya Aurora Madan and Debbie Smith; Shirley Manson's sharp-edged and glittering goth-glam; the untidy refusenik stylings of Bis's Manda Rin; and Skunk Anansie's Skin, whose concept of 'clit rock' was more compelling than the media's reductive and sensationalist presentation of her as an 'angry black lesbian' suggested. Catatonia's Cerys Matthews, whose lyrics and delivery mixed blowsy and raw-throated rockchickisms with an incisive sensitivity, catalogued her addictions, heartbreaks and disorders in a frank but delicate departure from the decade's flood of confessional art (which, aside from Richey James's contributions in *The Holy Bible*, largely flowed from female artists). Throughout the 90s, these voices were heard alongside those by whom they appear to have been retrospectively eclipsed, whether girl-power usurpers like the swiftly all-conquering Spice Girls, or unhelpful dullards like Sleeper, whose chosen presentation and marketing made them a better fit with Britpop hegemony: women with just enough agency to assert their right to appear on the cover of *Loaded*.

The adoption and discarding by Damon Albarn, as exemplar, of stereotyped Cockney or Essex trappings in which he lacked experience or investment, and the infestation of 90s music, film, art and media with equivalent *faux*-proles, would have been less bothersome had so many of them not played on the fondly imagined sexism and chauvinism of the 'lower orders' to express such attitudes themselves, enlisting an identity in which unreconstructed or irresponsible attitudes could be performed while one's 'real' identity remained untainted. Much of the success of new laddism rested on this performative doublethink, which, as John Beynon has argued, involved not the celebration but the exploitation of a caricatured white working-class masculinity by an overwhelmingly middle-class cultural industry.[20] The logic of this, again, relied on the neoliberal and Blairite idea that class was no longer of consequence or significance, and that working-class identity expressly no longer held currency: if we were indeed all middle-class now, then who could possibly be insulted or offended by seeing themselves stereotyped for fun and profit like this? This attempt to render the actual working class politically invisible, while their cultural artefacts were ironically adopted, sat uncomfortably with the lived experience of much of the country. Neither did it entirely fit with the fetish made of the working-class 'authenticity' of Oasis – an assertion of credibility based not on occupational categories but more on a generic perception of the Gallagher brothers' 'humble, ordinary' origins outside London and their excitingly 'difficult' family background. The valorising of authenticity in popular music, via its equation with a 'folk voice' identified with working-class experience, meant that the high incidence of postmodern shallowness in Blur's aesthetic and performance automatically devalued them when set against the presumed northern grit of Oasis, even though the straightforward swagger of Liam Gallagher's delivery was as much a performative choice as the mannered style of Albarn.

The 1995 chart battle between Oasis and Blur was heavily framed as one of social, aesthetic and regional oppositions: North versus South, duffel-coated Manc lads-made-good versus foppish Home Counties artschool loafers, and, above all, working class versus middle class. The *Daily Mail* was typical, and perhaps more perceptive than it knew, in interpreting the eventual win for Blur's Country House as 'The Pop Victory That Makes It Hip To Be Middle Class'. In reality, the class presentation of both bands was hopelessly compromised: the Gallaghers were not from quite as mean a Mancunian street as imagined, Blur's upbringings were not quite so uncomplicatedly cushioned as their accusers implied – but the identities claimed for both bands were equally unreconstructed, and both served to entrench the prevailing national discourse of beery retrograde chauvinism. The linking of Oasis' proletarian authenticity with loutish ignorance and excess was no less frustrating than the 'ironic', iconic soft sexism that defined Blur's video for Country House, on which Damon Albarn reflected: 'It worked, basically, because we used Page Three girls more than anything... it's worked because it has embraced the tabloid sentiment of what these last few weeks have been about'.[21] This both reinforced negative class stereotypes and contributed to the unedifying downturn in cultural discourse which was played out across the pages of the music press and liberal broadsheets as much as *Loaded* and the *Sun*. Noel Gallagher's disdain for Blur blended a class-conscious impulse with leaden machismo:

I really hate Damon... He thinks we're thick Northerners and he thinks everyone that buys our records are, like, idiots because they don't know the difference between Balzac and Prozac or whatever he's going on about... And the bass player's a closet faggot who wants his nose smacking in.[22]

This was counterbalanced by Albarn's presentation when interviewed for *Loaded* in 1994, in which he relished his unlikely rise from reading Nabokov (identified with middle-class pretension) to extolling the virtues of 'football, dog-racing and Essex girls'. Less tediously normative models of masculinity, whether Suede's early Bowieisms, the beta-male balladry of James, or the Manic Street Preachers' glam ambiguity and feminist sloganeering, were overridden by bands whose subscription to a certain eyelinered and skinny-tied model denoted few, if any, transgressive aspirations.[23] Overexcited lad culture increasingly eclipsed those who lacked or eschewed such contrivances, leaving little room for identities other than its straight, white, putatively 'working-class' (for which read unpretentious and intellectually incurious) cheerleaders of overextended adolescence.

For the restless, ambitious or otherwise dissatisfied working class, access to higher education, like the ability to excel in arts or sport, had traditionally offered a way out of 'chav-land'. This convention highlights the older inter-class designation of 'chavs' as an education-hostile and subsequently prospectless subculture, separate from those who claim respectability by virtue of their minds. This was the dividing line repeatedly drawn by Pulp's Jarvis Cocker, whose Britpop-era success as a chronicler of class antagonisms should not overshadow the degree to which his lyrics concentrate on working-class communities as something to escape rather than eulogise. In Mis-Shapes, Cocker definitively depicts the time-honoured antipathy of proto-'chav' (in the band's own parlance, 'townie') aggressors to the song's protagonists, sensitive intellectual youth who 'learned too much at school'. The song, as Owen Hatherley has written, 'lay[s] claim to working-class intelligence against the notion of class as mere identity and ethnicity, sportswear and accents, thuggery and racism'.[24] It also articulates the defensive, anomalous position such individuals can be made to feel they occupy, through the impression that such confounding blends of origin and intellect 'weren't supposed to be'. The liminal social and psychological space into which education can allow one to 'escape', its unsettled and unsettling quality, was noted by Richard Hoggart in *The Uses of Literacy*, observing the 'uprooted and anxious' nature of scholarship boys who, having secured some measure of cultural capital through education, gain social mobility at the expense of a secure class identity. Suede's Brett Anderson was similarly informed by the sense of rootlessness obtained as 'an educated, artistic kid from a working-class background':

> *I've never ever fitted into any stereotype... I wasn't part of an art-school clique...You know, my dad was a taxi driver, I'm from a very working class background, but not a conventional working class background. That's where the constant references in songs to these sort of nowhere places, comes from, because I never really felt that I belonged anywhere.*[25]

Inhabitants of this no-man's-land fought a losing battle for space in much 90s popular culture. After New Labour's commendable if compromised drive towards expansion of higher education as a means to social mobility, and the subsequent explosion of that aspiration by the present coalition's education policies, it is easy to lose sight of less strictly mercenary views of education. Rather than merely constituting a direct line to future economic profit, the 'adding of value' to an individual, it can offer a route out to broader social and cultural horizons, with the economic benefits which might thereby accrue only a secondary consideration. For men like the veteran Labour MP and former coalminer Dennis Skinner, the pit offered a 'second education' through a day-release scheme to college to study political theory, economics and industrial relations.[26] What now seems a fairly quaint emphasis on education as an agreeable means of self-improvement, and a means of salvation from a less desirable workerist fate, still informed the Manic Street Preachers' Richey James in 1993 when recounting his class-inflected experience of university, and underlining the varying conceptualisations of 'work', as a product of deindustrialised south Wales:

> *I went there to study, to learn. I went there to avoid work, to avoid manual labour... All these students who sat around saying 'I worked really hard today, I read loads'. That's not what I'd classify as work. It was going to a nice library and reading books all day. That was a pleasure and a privilege... I despised those people who sat in the bar going, 'Oooh, I was really rebellious today, I didn't go to one lesson!' When you think of the people who would dearly love to go to university, and then these idiots turn it into a joke... Public schoolboys drinking loads of lager and having a big fight, all these stupid fights between the rowing club and the rugby squad - It's frightening, because these people end up with the best jobs...[27]*

The tradition which prized education rather than despising it on the one hand, or taking it for granted on the other, was predicated upon the consciousness of gaining access to cultural and social capital previously denied on grounds of class, and has not been entirely eradicated from working-class psychology. The Manic Street Preachers were, before most other things, preposterous and anomalous, their class identity standing in obvious opposition to Blur's concocted Essexisms, but equally distinct from both Pulp's artschool/suburbia alignment and Suede's sink estate operatics. Their brand of Bevanite, Scargillite, workingmen's club socialism gained its most iconic expression in the 1996 class requiem Design for Life, in particular the stately opening salvo ('Libraries gave us power') and the scourging self-parody of the chorus, but it was present to a less explicit degree throughout most of the band's career. Although *The Holy Bible* intersected with the 90s cultural turn towards individualist ways of expressing socio-political discontent, a large part of the album's power is derived from the tension between this confessional, solipsistic tendency and the band's roots in older collectivist forms of protest and resistance. In 1998 the Manics' SYMM, a perhaps mawkish remembrance of the Hillsborough dead, nevertheless provided a necessary indictment of how the state, police, and media institutionalised fear and distrust of mass working-class engagement, leading to football crowds being caged and corralled – a practice foreshadowing the prevalence at later protests of techniques like kettling. (The song certainly managed to be marginally more edifying than, from the same year, Fat Les's Vindaloo.) And, as early as 1993's Gold Against the Soul, the weary stoicism of the line 'working-class clichés start here / either cloth caps or smack victims' did as much to anticipate the twenty-first century as to sum up the late twentieth. In the 90s cultural and political mainstream, this kind of class sentiment was received as a baffling throwback, less palatable, and certainly requiring harder work to understand, than either the cartoon-punk outrage of S*M*A*S*H or Oasis' lumpen-aspirational *braggadocio*.

The proletarian scholar, emblematic of the fact that intellectual capacity and personal potential can be influenced but not dictated by socioeconomic background, appeared nowhere in the Britpop roll call of class caricatures. Such a figure would have complicated the determinist dichotomy whereby Oasis, as representatives of the working class, could be presented as oafish, uneducated and semi-criminal, while Blur, as representatives of the middle class, could be equally automatically considered overeducated aesthetes. The decisive rise of Oasis, and the associated promotion of heart-and-soul 'real music' over experimentation, wit, or political engagement, dovetailed with a culture similarly suspicious of intellectualism, and a revived tabloid chauvinism, driven largely by the middle-class and well-educated, which promoted the kind of negative or comic class associations that many working-class people concerned themselves with striving to disprove or shake off. The element of cultural exploitation involved in Cool Britannia, its proponents playing at being authentic exponents of a class they simultaneously sneered at and sentimentalized, would be repeated *ad nauseam* in the decade to come. Hence the continued resonance of Pulp's Common People, a 1995 single as much about the stifled dreams, narrow horizons, and frustrated (not necessarily wasted) potential of its eponymous heroes as about the appropriative antics of its anti-heroine. The song's magnificent contempt for holidays in other people's misery, also displayed by the Manic Street Preachers towards those they encountered upon entering the music industry who thought taking drugs was 'the height of hedonism and depravity... They need to spend some time with the working classes, that would wipe the smile off their faces', could do little to stem the tide of class appropriation as the 90s washed into the 00s, where these excitingly transgressive indicators of an anti-intellectual, downwardly-mobile identity shaded increasingly into 'chav' drag.

Wear high heels and get a record deal and you won't have time to be sad

'To be natural is such a very difficult pose to keep up.'
- Oscar Wilde, *An Ideal Husband*

'I just thought it was better to be Pete Best than Linda McCartney.'
- Justine Frischmann (Elastica) on her departure from Suede

Like 'chav', 'feminism' is a powerful political tool. In the cultural skirmishes of the early 90s, the transformation of the independent scene into money-spinning 'indie' took place around the same time as an odd concordance of feminism and neoliberalism, in which the former's relationship with capitalism moved from critique towards accommodation. Neoliberal ideas of individual agency, of choice and self-sufficiency, found expression in 90s popular culture in the bright, peppy and profitable 'girl power' most visibly associated with the Spice Girls, to whom the hegemonic torch was swiftly passed around 1996 as Britpop began to lose its grip. For women in indie, as in other areas of popular culture, expressions of alternative, often politicised identities gave way throughout the decade to a manufactured and consumerist expression of postfeminist individualism. The early 90s had been heavily influenced by not only grunge but also riot grrrl, a DIY activist subculture closely aligned both with the aftershocks of punk and with frustration with postfeminism. Musician and activist Tobi Vail, credited as one of the scene's pioneers, recalled in 2009:

At the end of the 90s, The Spice Girls' watered-down version of 'girl power' had me questioning whether there was a place for real independent women in mainstream pop culture, not to mention the

effectiveness of the early-90s riot-grrrl movement in the face of this
blatant co-option of our terminology.[28]

Like their cultural sister Carrie Bradshaw and her self-expression through shopping and fucking, the Spice Girls purveyed an enervated and complacent feminism perfectly in tune with the prevailing inclination towards consumerism and individualism. Their exhortation that 'girls can do anything!' left no room for attention to the structural reasons why some girls were less empowered than others. This kind of power-feminism, as Rebecca Hains has noted, 'assumes that girls are empowered from the get-go, needing only to use their inherent power to affect change'.[29] Feminism's co-option by neoliberalism saw its focus of examination move from wider society to the individual, with analyses of inability to achieve or progress accordingly shifting from structural inequalities to personal failings of determination or ambition. This shift echoed the neoliberal insistence that we inhabit a meritocracy which excludes the possibility of disadvantage based on gender, race, class or sexuality: if you haven't got it, therefore, you must simply not have tried sufficiently hard or wanted it enough. A function of such disconnected thinking was the elevation of highly achieving women as models of personal empowerment and attainment, regardless of what their achievements consisted of. So Natasha Walter's *The New Feminism*, for instance, could describe Margaret Thatcher as an 'unsung heroine' of British feminism who 'normalised female success', ignoring the negative material effects of Thatcher's policies on other women.[30] This fracturing of joined-up feminist thought was the backdrop to Geri Halliwell's ominous assertion in 1997 that 'Margaret Thatcher was the first Spice Girl, the pioneer of our ideology', a quote of useful idiocy which made the headlines even though Halliwell's more thoughtful co-vocalists cringed.

Whereas riot grrrl had focused on interrogating and

challenging prescribed feminine identities through strategies of disruption and subversion, by scrawling SLUT or UGLY on exposed skin, reclaiming or questioning sexually derogatory terms and identities, the big female names of 90s mainstream-aspirant indie were increasingly presented and received through the reactionary paradigms of burgeoning lad culture. The alleged brains behind the website Chavspotting, identifying the contrived and marketing-led nature of the 'girl power' brand, also identify it as 'the first time that females properly embraced chavdom' – a claim based on the licence it granted 'ugly talentless slappers' to indulge in heavy drinking and town-centre brawling.[31] (It's here, perhaps, that James Delingpole's night terrors begin to raise their pasty-faced, Lambrini-addled heads from the gutter.) This reading of 'girl power' did in fact blend easily with the 'ladette' identity, in which single-minded devotion to boorish excess was seldom troubled by any more all-encompassing egalitarian impulse, with little suggestion that women could be equal to men in arenas other than that of competitive pint-downing. Sleeper's strikingly cynical Louise Wener, one of Britpop's best-remembered pin-ups, developed a strategy of being 'provocative, rebellious and print-worthy' in order to garner attention as a female player in the 'anachronistic and ghettoised arena' of the 90s music press.[32] This rebellion, however, took the form of a tedious soft-right sneering at feminism and political correctness, which, rather than constituting daring contrarianism, merely offered a self-serving capitulation to new laddism. Sleeper's songs dealt with the generic Britpopisms of suburban and domestic tedium interrupted by excursions into sex and booze, but their protagonists seemed wholly incapable of taking genuine pleasure in the process. For all Wener's hiccupy attempts at titillation, Sleeper were an oddly coy and prudish band, try-hard where Kenickie were effortless, lacking Elastica's languorous seediness or the exhilarated malevolence of

Shampoo, and painting a curious portrait of the ladette as joylessly dutiful housewife.

Justine Frischmann, whose instrumental part in Britpop's foundation remains undersung, formed Elastica in 1992 after having co-founded, managed and then left Suede for her iconic power-coupling with Damon Albarn. Although pulled along by the Britpop undertow, Elastica were an oddity within it: uninterested in Beatles/Stones reanimation, they were more the only notable survival of New Wave of New Wave, rooted in 70s rather than 60s recycling. Their phenomenally successful 1995 debut, with its stripped down, angular art-punk, its odd, listless mix of sleaze and melancholy, and the band's Last Gang In Town fronting on photoshoots and record sleeves, anticipated the revival of such stylings almost a decade later by the Strokes/Libertines axis of hipster. Their aesthetic sharpened by the urchin edge of Frischmann's musical foil Donna Matthews, Elastica adopted a new wave uniform of black leather jackets, skinny jeans and boyish haircuts, a protective covering which further allowed them to avoid or subvert a certain degree of objectification. Like their all-women frontline, this pleasingly complicated Elastica's heavy musical debt to the Stranglers and Wire (the band's unabashed plagiarism, or open acknowledgement of their influences, was hardly more egregious than, say, Oasis's borrowings from T-Rex, Slade and the Glitter Band). In songs like the withering Stutter, the itchily impatient All-Nighter or the archly lascivious Car Song, Frischmann expressed a coolly assertive, even emasculating sexual agency, her playfully frank lyrics and nonchalant blurring of gender norms sometimes suggesting a southern female mirror-image of Buzzcocks' Pete Shelley. Her lyrics were steeped in detached self-possession and delivered in a dry, campy *Sprechgesang* which betrayed little in the way of messy emotion. There was 'just' sex in the majority of these songs, little sentiment and less romance, but there was equally little angst, judgement or self-reproach.

For Frischmann, her androgynous aesthetic was a deliberate response to her perception of the vulnerability that femininity could signify, an attempt to deflect attention using what she described as 'Nineties urban camouflage':

> When you're in your twenties you feel more confident about what you are, you don't feel like you necessarily have to dress up for boys … If you're wearing long hair and make-up, you're gonna feel a lot more vulnerable than if you've got short hair and big boots.[33]

This 'tomboy' persona was not exactly that of the pre-eminent media 'ladette'. It also ran counter to the manufactured tomboyism of the Spice Girls' Mel C, whose imposed persona, in tracksuits and scraped-back ponytail, was a fairly precise simulation of the modern 'chav' at a point when these signifiers were less straightforwardly derogatory. Frischmann explained her androgynous self-presentation as 'just expecting to be treated as one of the lads. You don't want to deliberately remove yourself from being able to be a good bloke'. The music press, however, invariably associated Frischmann with her boyfriends past and present ('hair by Brett, boots by Damon'), both denying her any creative agency and actually inverting the dynamic of her contribution to both Blur and Suede. The received wisdom of Britpop as a male concern and male preserve obscures how highly-rated Elastica were at the time – notably, they came closer than either Oasis or Blur to cracking the lucrative US market – and it also overlooks the contribution made by Frischmann to Britpop's originating impulse.

That the media insistently presented Justine Frischmann in relation to the men she chose to sleep with was part of a wider sexualisation whereby, in the post-Britpop 90s, women's sexual agency had increasingly to be offered within a Lad frame of reference. Her sexually confident persona and Elastica's pleasure-centred lyrics, despite their matter-of-fact delivery, tended to be treated as naughtily, haughtily deviant departures from feminine convention, rather than just another way in which women might view themselves and their sex lives. It's tempting to conclude that Frischmann's ostensibly aloof and independent approach, her chilled assertiveness, and her androgyny, not to mention her openness about her well-off family background in the era of 'poor is cool', attracted a reductive emphasis on her sexuality and sex life as a way of rendering her comprehensible, less of a threat and more of a 'regular girl'. It worked awkwardly within the overall regressive climate, from Frischmann's unrelenting and frequently disingenuous sexualisation by the music press and wider media to Liam Gallagher's taking her casual mention of *Playboy* as a pretext to enjoin her publicly to 'get your tits out'. Her eventual break-up with Albarn in 1997 was partly the result of her reluctance to accept what she perceived as the restrictions of domesticity and motherhood. For Blur themselves, internal tensions between progressive indie ideals and imperial-Britpop machismo were exemplified by Graham Coxon's relationship with Brighton riot grrrl Jo Johnson, whose dislike of Alex James' boorish excess was dismissed by the latter as 'right-onness'.[34] Johnson's band Huggy Bear, in their resolutely uncommercial music, anti-corporate stance, and subscription to the 'humourless feminism' of riot grrrl, were regarded as a last gasp of politically correct joylessness, to be rightfully abandoned with the rest of the 80s. Alongside this resurgent and largely unchallenged chauvinism, the prevailing materialist, individualist and image-led brand of 'girl power' was promoted as a depoliticised, nonthreatening and profitable form of feminism, a recuperation which not only displaced the explicitly politicised woman-centred music of riot grrrl but also edged out other pre-existing alternative and less commercial expressions of femininity.

Good taste is death, vulgarity is life: Shampoo and Kenickie

'To perceive Camp in objects and persons is to understand Being-as-Playing-a-Role. It is the farthest extension, in sensibility, of the metaphor of life as theatre... The experiences of Camp are based on the great discovery that the sensibility of high culture has no monopoly upon refinement.'
– Susan Sontag, 'Notes on Camp', 1964

'If anyone's manufacturing us, it's ourselves. We knew what we wanted and set out to meet the people who could help us create it – a raw punky glamorous band.'
– Jacqui Blake (Shampoo)[35]

Achieving the 'correct' kind of femininity has never been easy for women in the public eye, and their presentation is further complicated by issues of class. Kenickie, a 90s pop-aspirational indie band with wit, swagger and style to spare, were on one level examples of Delingpole's 'pasty-faced, lard-gutted slappers' too. Both they and Shampoo, a mock-delinquent duo from the London suburb of Plumstead, seemed more fully their own created cartoon, more at home in their proto-'chav' drag, than Jessie J or Lily Allen later appeared. Contemporary interviews often found half-baffled, half-seduced middle-class male journalists in awe of the bands' offstage inhabiting of their onstage personae: rather than stereotypes of exoticised others, they were opting to play the pantomime versions of themselves. Both Shampoo and Kenickie were grounded in appreciation of the Manic Street Preachers' escapist proletarian-glam aesthetic, both were able to articulate the experiences of suburban or provincial girls in fearless, loving awe of what the city and the future had to offer, and both embodied one music writer's identification of 'that terrifying stage where teenage girls are half-human, half-rat'.[36]

Shampoo, remembered mostly for the bubblegum-punk perfection of their third single Trouble, were snottily disdainful of anyone over twenty-one and of anyone 'still hanging out in Camden Town'. Jacqui Blake and Carrie Askew (their individual names seemed secondary to the impenetrable united front they presented) were informed by protective self-parody rather than stereotype, pouting and glowering in clashing styles and colours, a kitsch riot of fluorescent wigs, peroxide, high ponytails, dark sunglasses, animal print and glitter. Their songs were equally cartoonish, an escapist anatomy of the inane and mundane, staying out all night and staggering home at dawn to face the music, 'running wild in the city' and, in a line of splendidly evocative economy, 'throwing up your kebab in a shiny taxi cab'. Hyper and combative where Elastica were laid-back, Shampoo's music and image nevertheless evinced a similar kind of unimpressed and half-amused self-possession, offering no entry point for the vulnerability of sentiment or idealism. Their defensive, misfit outsiderdom lent itself to laconic lyrical viciousness: on Dirty Old Love Song they casually skewered the very clichés which teenage girls were meant to swallow whole, and Skinny White Thing derided proto-hipster culture with all the bored, bitchy observational accuracy of the playground and the small-town shopping centre sharpened into cutting critique. 'Girl power', before that term's hijacking by the Spice Girls, had featured in the work of Swansea Ramones-botherers Helen Love, a band whose finest moment was to be Long Live the UK Music Scene, a 1998 reel around Britpop's funeral pyre. Girl Power was also the title of Shampoo's 1995 second album and its lead single. Although they were by this point a major label novelty act, Shampoo's dour and dead-eyed anthem of 'girl power' as license for antisocial truculence ('I don't wanna go to college, don't wanna get a job', 'I wanna smash the place up just for fun') stood instructive comparison with the Spice Girls' tamed and defanged brand of empowerment through consumerism, as well as merrily mocking contemporary anxieties over female delinquency.

Kenickie began, like Elastica, as three girls with guitars and an unassuming boy drummer, forming in Sunderland in the summer of 1994. Like the Manics before them and the Libertines after them, Kenickie oozed Last Gang in Town glamour, but theirs was a distinctly girl gang: sticky cocktails and stick-on spangles rather than spilled pints and regrettable tattoos. Their acknowledgement of Courtney Love as a basis for their blend of charity shop chic and highstreet fashion also indicates the ways in which they extended the lessons of riot grrrl beyond that scene's demographic. Kenickie excelled at anatomising female self-loathing in its biological and social forms, and at fashioning sleek, fierce paeans to poised and self-possessed female independence. Where Shampoo were wilfully dumb and impenetrably obnoxious in their music and presentation, Kenickie offered greater intricacy, sympathy, intrigue and vulnerability. Their songs were full of the competing impulses of self-belief and self-doubt that blight adolescence, each presented in its respective natural habitat: streetlight-bright and PVC-shiny nights out with no coats on versus shadowy dawns full of shivering sleepless regret. The music, like the subject matter, ranged from brash and upfront to achingly romantic to grittily bleak, mixing spiky guitars and shiny blasts of brass with silvery swirls of keyboard and girl-group harmonies and handclaps. And they were as unapologetically sharp, witty and smart as they were sexy. In a teenage world stuck for role models between the Spice Girls' sham sisterhood and Sleeper's smug potshots at suburban cliché, Kenickie's attitude and aesthetic, as well as their music, did as much to outline my potential agency and autonomy as any feminist tome or broadsheet editorial I read.

The London music press tended to hymn Kenickie to the skies, as though the capacity of regional-accented girls for wit and articulacy came as some surprise. The band themselves, however, experienced their representation as a site of struggle. As purveyors of a regional and class-infused feminine identity, Kenickie complicated attempts by the music industry and media to fit them into accepted and appropriate boxes, and lost out in the process. Their guitarist and vocalist Marie Nixon recalls: 'Because we were girls, we had to be marketed as pop. No one would have ever asked our male contemporaries, like Ash, to model sunglasses on the Lorraine Kelly programme'.[37] In the music press and the wider industry, Kenickie's novelty status as 'northern lasses' led to an anxious objectification based on their perceived 'tartiness' – which, according to their bassist Emma Jackson, stemmed from a confused, because class-inflected, reading of the band's presentation:

> We realised the importance of the visual and from our inception tried to look 'glamorous', in our own way. We favoured short skirts, high heels and synthetic fibres - preferably in an animal print, celebrating our idea of glamour... It became obvious that EMI had worries about our image, whispers about 'tartiness' began to reach the band and increasingly stylists seemed to be steering us towards the knitwear sections in shops. Our maxim 'We dress cheap, we dress tacky' was now a commercial problem. Visually, our rather aggressive northern femininity, which was part of our appeal, had to be watered down.[38]

Kenickie's brassy, breezy self-expression was also presumed to signify an 'easy' sexuality, making them the objects of an unstable mixture of lust and disgust:

> We were asked if we were in anyway like Viz's Fat Slags, 'only thinner', and these were the journalists who liked us! The inter-

viewers seemed bemused by our hostility to their question - 'So what you're asking us, then, is, are we slags?' replied Lauren [Laverne, vocalist/guitarist] coolly. The asking of such a question demonstrates the reduction of all their assumptions about our perceived class, gender and regional roots to the grotesque parody of North East women in the Fat Slags comic strip. This ignored our own statements about our identity in our music.[39]

This lack of understanding by a middle-class media of how such a comparison might be received takes us back to the intersection of sexism and classism discussed in the first chapter, whereby all women who are perceived as working-class are implicitly 'chavs', and all 'chavs' are explicitly easy. Kenickie's female frontline, like Shampoo, had an earthy, cartoon-glam aesthetic: half Old Hollywood starlets, half explosion in Claire's Accessories. Their particular brand of glamour was, as Susan Sontag wrote of Camp, 'a variant of sophistication but hardly identical with it'. Their towering heels, aggressively revealing outfits and lashings of makeup were worn on their own terms; a Pink Ladies-inspired protective covering rather than a puppeteered provocation.

Tangled up with the roots of this look was the history of glamour as a means for 'ordinary' girls to dress 'above their station' through artifice, lavish and luxurious but popularly accessible, which did not require the backing of 'good breeding'. In its more recent forms, this kind of glamour has become identified as either 'vulgar' appropriation or defiant class drag, in both cases serving to emphasise rather than disguise the class of its wearer. Carol Dyhouse's history of the term, however, traces how glamour's possibilities for transcending class and gender barriers generated predictable anxiety, cloaked in snobbery and appeals to national loyalty: at the height of 'glamour' as emulative and ambitious artifice and excess, a signifier of the upwardly-mobile and autonomous woman 'on the make', British *Vogue* encouraged its female readership to forsake this brash, democratic and over-the-top aesthetic in favour of a 'natural English look'.[40]

Kenickie's songs were suffused with the idea of harnessing the escapist, aspirational glamour of the Night Out, using its imaginative appeal to transcend the grime and gloom in which one finds oneself immured. Their music offered a presentation of provincial female life crafted with sympathy and solidarity, and an insistence upon their social and sexual agency. This self-expression, coded as 'cheap' and 'tacky' but also constituting a sociologically specific idea of empowerment through glamour, was interpreted by outsiders as 'tarty', imparting a certain vulgar showiness, forwardness and immodesty, a judgement based on the band's perceived working-classness and on their deviation from hegemonic feminine conventions. Subtly but significantly different from ladettism, whose template was a doe-eyed and football-shirted take on the *gamine* rather than the glamour girl's campy excess and abundance, Kenickie's was not an identity which sat comfortably within Britpop. Like the figure of the working-class aesthete or politicised intellectual, the working-class girl who expressed a casually confident, self-possessed and independent sexuality on her own terms rather than those of lad culture struggled to find a respected place in the Britpop pantheon, even as Blur's video for Country House enlisted glamour models to portray working-class women's sexuality, under male direction, in the form of commodified stereotypes.

2.3 00s
Merrie England is mine, it owes me a living: Barât and Doherty

'Has there ever been a musician of cultural significance who's been aware they're significant? Maybe it's a generation whose parents came from a working class environment and because they were rootless in a way, like me and him, they latched onto that as an identity. Maybe we romanticise what our parents wanted to escape from. We're, like, fantasising out a living.'
– Peter Doherty (The Libertines), 2004

By the early 2000s 'indie' seemed to be losing many of its formerly distinguishing features. As the independent sector bowed to commercial imperatives and mainstream business models, its 'alternative' veneer became a marketing tool and the 'indie' label was rendered largely meaningless, defined at its most basic as whatever happened to be on the *NME's* cover on any given week. Boundaries between indie and pop, and between alternative and mainstream, had been collapsed by Britpop and were now decisively kicked aside. Successful millennial bands like Coldplay and Travis found themselves able to expand onto international stages by bleaching out 'British' idiosyncrasies and parochialisms in favour of increasingly bland and introspective universalisms. In wider culture, political discourse continued to drift lazily rightwards while insisting on the existence of liberal harmony and contentment in the face of worsening material inequality, leaving society becalmed in deepening waters of unfocused resentment and dissatisfaction. The size, diversity and militancy of popular opposition to the US-led war on Iraq, expressed throughout 2003 in some of the biggest mass demonstrations for a generation, made its subsequent dismissal by the Blair government all the more demoralising. The anti-war movement's dispirited evaporation, owing to issues of leadership and strategy as well as to the obduracy of a head of state inexorably wedded to military action, disillusioned many for whom it had been their first active experience of protest.

As the country's headlong political and economic dash back into the maw of the 80s demanded some kind of countercultural renewal, indie offered only a weak reanimation of the 90s Scene That Celebrates Itself, as the music industry and media tried manfully to resuscitate the excitement of a decade earlier. The 00s saw a rapid turnover of Londoncentric 'scenes', with varying degrees of cooperation, manipulation and resistance from the bands and audiences involved, and with the arena of antici-pation largely displaced from Camden to the art-squats, galleries, clubs and warehouse conversions of rapidly gentri-fying East London. Those receiving most attention were those who self-consciously courted it; Razorlight's Johnny Borrell, for one, was notable for a degree of aspiration that was almost painful to observe, his talent stretched just about sufficiently thin to cover his naked ambition. Beyond nods towards the anodyne, consumer-focused activism of Fairtrade campaigns, and the stalwarts of Love Music Hate Racism, a spirit of collective apathy and individualism prevailed, growing increas-ingly nostalgic through immersion in 'vintage' and 'retro' and increasingly reluctant to engage politically, when a superficial reading of events appeared to reinforce the idea of activism as futile and escapism as both an attractive and logical alternative. The embarrassing earnestness and vital vulgarity that fuelled early-90s indie still found flashes of inspiration in bands like ska-punks the King Blues, or contrarian folk-punks the Indelicates, a band both reliably irreverent and unhampered by the fear of being seen to mean it, but it was otherwise consumed by ironic detachment or wholesale disengagement.

In several otherwise demoralised surveys of the post-Britpop scene, including the afterword to John Harris's Britpop chronicle *The Last Party*, the Libertines were lit upon as constituting a belated passing of the torch. The Manic Street Preachers' Nicky Wire spoke admiringly of the band as exponents of rock'n'roll glamour and mythology (presumably the most vital example of the type since the Manics had ceased to be one themselves). The hype which consequently attached to the Libertines has tended in retrospect to overshadow more briefly interesting bands which occupied the same orbit: Luxembourg's pop-noir, the freakbeat of Neil's Children, Art Brut's deadpan minimalism, the Chris Morris-inspired Snow White's seethingly misanthropic punk-metal, or Patrick Wolf and Lupen Crook's focus on the dark side of Doherty's moon-faced adulation of urban squalor. The Libertines adopted a cynically simple approach to building their own trajectory within a tradition of iconic British rock, tying themselves to the coat-tails of the Smiths, the Jam, the Clash, and their echoes in early pale-and-interesting Britpop, as much by their compulsively ramshackle live performances and Last Gang in Town self-mythologizing as by their fateful installing of Britpop kingpin Alan McGee as manager. Peter Doherty's short reign as poster-boy for unedifying excess has immortalised his band more as a footnote to the crash and burn of their most volatile component than for their more interesting qualities.

The Libertines were large and contained multitudes. They bear comparison with Oasis in as much as they were unarguably a cut above the multiple copyists who rushed in to fill the vacuum left by their self-destruction. The band revolved around the alchemical partnership of Doherty and his co-frontman, the underrated black-dogged matinée idol Carl Barât (their rhythm section, relentlessly affable drummer Gary Powell and Merseybeat-obsessive bassist John Hassall, seemed to have wandered in from another band altogether). Barât and Doherty's 2000 showcase *Legs XI* was an intriguing and endearing rag-bag of romantic nostalgia, its music magpied from skiffle, skank, barbershop and music-hall, its lyrics rehabilitating more thoughtful aspects of Englishness than those Britpop had bothered with, like the interwar class realism of Walter Greenwood's *Love on the Dole*, offering a blend of class signifiers which tended to sentimentalise more than they mocked. The Libertines' subsequent leap aboard the Strokes-informed bandwagon, along with a clutch of bands melding millennial Britpop with brittle and angular retro-garage, did not change the messily fashioned longing in their *oeuvre* and aesthetic for a half-imagined past which merged Ealing comedy with poetry in the trenches and an ideal of giddy London hedonism.

Barât and Doherty's foundation myth, invoking epic, intimate and escapist romance and soulmateship, marked a self-conscious but nonetheless refreshing departure from lad rock masculinity. The knowingly homoerotic charge between both frontmen, and Doherty's nonchalant declarations of pansexu-ality – in addition, less happily, to Barât's subjection to an extra-ordinary level of inter-band, media and audience objectification – made them seem as much of a relief as the emphatic machismo of Oasis had been almost a decade earlier. (The notable overlap between Libertines fans and former fans of the Manic Street Preachers, whose early 'all rock'n'roll is homosexual' posturing made them the last significant standard bearers for pre-Britpop models of masculinity, may indicate this strategy's effec-tiveness.) Despite a regrettable poetic penchant for 'pale thin girls', Doherty also evinced a notable attachment in lyrics and in real life to sparky, independent women: on his 2009 solo work *Grace/Wastelands*, 'the last of the English roses' is pint-swilling and politically astute, and how pale, thin and eyes-forlorn she is we neither know nor care. She has a precursor in Campaign of Hate's 'Sharleen', who is aggressively witty, sexually voracious and more than a match for (one of) the boys. These sparks of subversion leavened the otherwise wince-worthy retro-chauvinism lurking in the likes of Boys in the Band, which was nodded through by a depoliticised wider culture accustomed to assuming the kind of automatic, all-encompassing irony which obviated offence. Deeply performative, Boys in the Band in fact spoke as much of resentful insecurity as it did of the assurance to be found by adopting the mantle of rock'n'roll machismo; underneath this, the song's protagonist, having 'no homestead' and 'jealous of my own', is as restless, lost and despondent as Hoggart's anxious and uprooted scholarship boys. Significantly perhaps, Doherty's upbringing featured both a series of army garrisons and a comprehensive school at which he excelled academically; Barât, the product of an 'unpopular' childhood, split between arts-and-crafts bohemia and a Basingstoke council estate, and a 'disappointing' studenthood, 'liked to think of himself as self-educated working-class, though he knew it didn't tell the whole story'.[41] Campaign of Hate contains a casual but sharp summation of cultural appropriation, approvingly referencing Mod as 'poor kids dressing like they're rich' before comically despairing of rich kids dressing like they're poor.

The offstage indulgence and onstage personality clashes which formed a cornerstone of the Barât and Doherty legend, and which tend to take centre stage in Libertines retrospectives, obscure the wealth of cultural references employed by the band, as well as the progressive political impulse attached to them. Central to this was the concept of Albion and Arcadia, which recur in Libertines interviews and lyrics as a vaguely sketched inclusive ideal, filtered through Doherty's absorbing of Michael Bracewell's idiosyncratic pop history *England Is Mine* (1997). Despite the frequency of right-wing populist co-options of a romantic-nostalgic vision of England, the Libertines looked back to Albion and Arcadia rather as they figure in the proto-communist visions of Blake and the early critiques of commercial capitalism by John Ruskin, William Morris and

Robert Blatchford. Much of their 2002 debut *Up the Bracket* attempts to transplant *Merrie England's* agrarian communism to a mock-Dickensian urban utopia – where it functions as an ideal to be attained collectively, perhaps, but by substance-fuelled escape into the realm of the imagination, Rimbaud's 'systematic derangement of the senses', rather than through direct action. The album's supporting single Time for Heroes is probably the best case in point of the Libertines' political limitations. Retrospectively extolling London's anti-globalisation riots of May Day 2001, the song forges its own mythology of young bloods and obscene scenes, its lyrics rich with in-jokes, quietly camp wit and countercultural hat-tips (the arresting line 'Wombles bleed' refers not to Elisabeth Beresford's fictional creations but to the riot's attendance by the anarchist group of the same name). Doherty's invocation of 'ignorant faces that bring this town down', and the peerless line 'there are fewer more distressing sights than that of an Englishman in a baseball cap', tread similar ground to Cocker's delineation of a misfit, unacknowledged subset of the working class, a quasi-Wildean refusal of the expected signifiers of class identity as both ill-suited and aesthetically displeasing. The song's politics, though, are never quite brought into satisfactorily sharp relief, remaining a vaguely colourful backdrop to individual 'heroism', and this personalised trajectory overshadows the song's political perspective. The narrative is focused on the 'stylish kids'; the riot, apart from the edgy iconography and romantic associations it can supply, is incidental. The collectivist consciousness of Time for Heroes, in common with the rest of the band's reper-toire, remained an impulse which was easily abstracted and distilled into another signifier stripped of meaning, the equiv-alent of the *keffiyehs* frequently present around the necks of 00s scenesters who appeared bemused when asked for their views on Palestinian solidarity. The ramshackle romanticism of Barât and Doherty's utopian socialism was not enough to fully overcome the post-political apathy and solipsism which compromised their scene, nor to meaningfully reanimate signifiers so thoroughly emptied of import.

Predicting riots

'I don't get rock'n'roll. I don't get all that smashing up the hotel rooms. The next morning, someone's mum has to come and clean up afterwards. That's not rock'n'roll – rock'n'roll would be buying her a holiday'.
– Ricky Wilson (Kaiser Chiefs), 2008

The loss of what promise the Libertines held was sudden and sharp. The band finally splintered in 2004 on the release of their anticlimactic second album, and Barât and Doherty's largely lacklustre subsequent work proved their alliance had been greater than the sum of its parts, while their copyists and associates extended the band's most regressive and anti-intellectual aspects with none of their saving graces. The 90s revival which began to receive broadsheet attention some time in 2011 had been 'impending' for at least half of the preceding decade, as though being willed into existence by a culture in search of the last time it had something tangible to grasp. But, as indicated by the ex-Britpop Primrose Hill flotsam which collected around both the Libertines and Barât and Doherty's later efforts, the dead hand of the 90s never really let go, the decade's cultural detritus continually bobbing to the surface like something unflushable. In the twilight of New Labour, the dregs of 'second-wave Britpop' often seemed to have awkwardly forced Oasis' workmanlike musical substance together with the glib style of *Parklife*-era Blur, fashioning music made of bog-standard chauvinism given the disarming gloss of irony. The post-Oasis battening by record companies on the 'lad market', spawning both bands and music crafted with charmless cynicism, meant that 'indie' appeared to deliquesce into a decreasingly relevant puddle of male-exclusive bands with an increasingly reductive musical palette and a narrow class identity, again predicated on a stereotype of white and provincial working-class masculinity modelled on the late-Britpop template of birds, beer and being content with your lot. Reinforcing the idea that working-classness in a band, or an audience, equates to being incapable of engaging with a greater level of nuance or sophistication than that contained in meat-and-potatoes guitar-rock, the majority of lad rock bands lyrically embraced the mundanity of life in dead-end small towns in a manner that underlined the oddity of not doing so. While prolesploitation bands have commodified Oasis's 'authenticity', the accompanying urge to transcend or escape the confines imposed by one's background, an ambition fuelling far more of Oasis' early work than might be assumed from their imitators, seems as distant a tradition as the post-punk engagement with radicalism and innovation which galvanized artists from Mark E. Smith to the Manics.

When indie bands weren't portraying the working class as stoical socioeconomic captives happily singing in their chain pubs, they were presenting them as monstrous opponents to whom the civilised had been forced to abandon the field of conflict. The Kaiser Chiefs' 2004 curio I Predict a Riot tended to recur in jokey responses to the London riots of August 2011, also surfacing as a deservedly dismissive allusion in the lyrics of Plan B's Ill Manors.[44] Perhaps this referencing only proves the cultural poverty of the intervening years, but it also demonstrates the song's longevity, far greater than that of its fast-obsolescing creators, and its enduring appeal as a checkpoint for class-inflected fear and loathing. Where Pulp in Mis-Shapes, and to an extent the Libertines in Time for Heroes, had complicated the idea of the working class as a homogenous ill-educated mass, invoking instead the persistence of cerebral and cultural engagement, in I Predict a Riot the line of separation is that of prurient disgust, degrees of sensibility rather than intellectual distinction or aspiration, with the 'chav' stereotype emerging as a convenient way to delineate divisions. This marked a subtle shift from the Britpop era, where working-class signifiers could be comically, enticingly, even aspirationally appropriated in the manner debunked by Common People. For Sheffield band Arctic Monkeys in A Certain Romance, sartorial class signifiers associated with 'chav' aggression ('classic Reeboks', 'tracky bottoms tucked in socks') could be more trenchantly summoned as part of a nuanced and sympathetic self-assessment before being dismissed as 'what the point is not', rather than inviting uncomprehending Amis-esque point-and-stare fear or condescension. For Ricky Wilson's protagonist, though, as for an increasing number of 00s commentators, they form part of a threatening and marginalised carnival of horrors, rendered almost alien.

The song's litany of Boschian frights encountered during the denouement of a Night Out also foreshadows Delingpole's invocation of working-class women as, lest we forget: 'gangs of embittered, hormonal, drunken teenagers… pasty-faced, lard-gutted slappers who'll drop their knickers in the blink of an eye…', a stone's throw away from Wilson's censorious, if timorous, reportage ('girls scrabble round with no clothes on to borrow a pound for a condom / if it wasn't for chip-fat they'd be frozen…'). Sneering by grammar-school boys at slatternly scrabbling for small change was perhaps the logical culmination of late Britpop's fellow-travelling new laddism, a tendency having waxed unapologetically blatant and boorish in the post-Libertines scene. Certainly by 2011, after the distancing minstrelsy of Fat Les's Vindaloo, the bathetic nudge-and-wink of Blur's Stereotypes, and 'we are all middle-class now', after Waynetta Slob and Vicky Pollard, these truths were held to be self-evident: the streets of darkest Britain delineated as a volatile, flammable under-kingdom haunted by spectres to whom junk-food is both fuel and insulation, track-suited thugs and girl-golems clad in chip-fat. These factors reflect a cultural shift which has combined the vanishing of working-class, and especially female working-class, identity in public discourse with its accelerated use as an all-purpose whipping-post for a host of social ills and moral panics. Something surely obvious over the past few years, but seemingly unremarked upon in the sudden panicked acknowledgement of contemporary indie as meaningless, mainstream, and moneyed, was how uniformly male the railed-against 'landfill' guitar bands were. What happened to the women, in particular the 90s phalanx of 'pasty-faced, lard-gutted slappers'?

If it jars to consider that an anthem of diminished indie like I Predict a Riot could soundtrack a trip into the tortured psyches of our most conservative cultural critics, it's even more jarring to recall the potential of early 90s indie, whose space for oddity allowed through voices which occasionally managed to be those of the chip-fat girls themselves. These were voices capable of non-hysterically narrating the Night Out from the perspective of celebrant, embedded insider rather than alarmed observer, presenting drunken scrabbling, one-night stands and non-sensible clothing as unremarkable rituals of growing up rather than the morally bankrupt bacchanalia for which working-class women are presently castigated. Outside the pop bubble, the past few years' 'chav'-hysteria, the pathologising of the Night Out, has enabled incessant media and political policing of the social, economic and sexual lives of young women via stereotypes of an unruly and irresponsible underclass. This, along with the remoteness of much mainstream feminist discourse, has shaped a scenario where working-class women appear mostly as externally designated objects of panic, ridicule, pity or contempt. Any cultural counterweight to this stereotype, any genuine alternative expression of lived experience, must struggle to breathe.

Fairytales in the supermarket

'Both black and white working-class women have historically been coded "as the sexual and deviant other against which femininity [is] defined"... their attempts to "do femininity" are often read as "a class drag act, an unconvincing and inadvertently parodic attempt to pass."'
– Beverley Skeggs, quoted in Imogen Tyler [43]

'Being derogatory about someone who's done well from nothing? That's hilarious, I love that. It's a big compliment — I'm a chav.'
– Cheryl Cole, 2012

The musical greywash and sidelining of women artists which occurred under late Britpop appeared to reach its dull conclusion in the late-00s profusion of almost invariably male 'landfill indie' groups. Even before this, a 2004 *NME* feature on the resurgent London scene, its accompanying photoshoot crammed with skinny jeans and skinnier ties, had only two women as participants.[44] Many women in the loose-knit scene which launched the Libertines not only appreciated the music surrounding them but were actively engaged in creating music, writing, poetry, art and fashion of their own. None of this was reflected in the mainstream media, who, training a sensationalist gaze on Peter Doherty, presented his female fans and associates, including the millionaire businesswoman Kate Moss, in conventionally passive and decorative roles: either gormless good-girl victims lured into crackdens of iniquity, or sexily wrecked bad-girl groupies who deserved all they got. This reassertion of a retro status quo – a kind of New Wave of New Laddism – with its downgrading of women's agency, blended uneasily with the 'ironic', performative versions of pre-60s femininity reclaimed or commodified in the fashions through which alternative/hipster culture rapidly cycled, from nu-folk to neo-burlesque and 'cupcake feminism'. The latter tendency formed part of a larger and on-going trend, in which traditional necessary domestic crafts were reconfigured as a kitsch lifestyle choice. The commendably subversive aspects of this tendency have, as ever, largely been lost in its translation to the mainstream, which has co-opted its riot grrrl-rooted signifiers while erasing its critique. This has left domestic chic vulnerable to accusations of eulogising a romanticised ideal of middle-class and white retro-femininity, unhelpfully amenable to adoption by a conservative discourse which encourages women to remain within the domestic sphere and whose policies restrict women's repro-ductive and employment rights.[45] In contrast to largely middle-class domestic chic, the 90s 'ladette' identity, retaining its conno-tations of disruptive boisterousness and obnoxious indepen-dence, seemed to transfer itself in 00s representations to the realm of working-class women, where it merged with 'chav' as a signifier of undesirable femininity to be proscribed and manipulated in popular discourse.

One mildly intriguing aspect of the 00s was the way in which 'chav' signifiers could be used to construct an affirmative identity, both by male artists like the Streets' Mike Skinner and by Lady Sovereign, a product of London's dilapidated Chalkhill Estate. On the 2006 single Love Me or Hate Me, Lady Sovereign mocks stereotypically feminine dress and mannerisms while the 'chav' identity, with its capacity for the effacement and challenging of conventional femininity, becomes a liberatory breathing-space for other forms of experimental self-expression. But this was of course also open to co-option and appropriation: Lady Sovereign received little of the mainstream acclaim granted to the less genuinely grimy Lily Allen, an early exponent both of *faux*-indie underground discovery and of chav-pop princessery. Her subsequent industry and media elevation was of course aided by the fact that Allen's background consisted not merely of her much-mentioned council estate but also the bohemian boarding school Bedales and Cool Britannia clagnut Keith Allen, a man made rich partly through entrenching the working-class as venal and risible comic relief in the national drama. Although capable of intriguing and endearing interior monologues, in articulating the experience she appropriates Allen is a similar safe class minstrel, symptomatic of British mainstream music's current pantomime in which representatives of the same class are able to play both princess and Cinderella.

The narratives woven around femininity in the mainstream media frequently orbit the same anxieties as those around 'chav', proscribing social and sexual agency and independence and promoting a neutered, caricatured version of female assertiveness. Like the concomitant forms of femininity, the forms of high-visibility celebrity available to working-class women are regulated and relentlessly disciplined. A specific form of this discipline arises in relation to what Imogen Tyler and Bruce Bennet have analysed as the 'celebrity chav', an 'abject, gauche and excessively tragi-comic' figure, invariably of working-class origin and usually female, one of whose defining features is an inability to 'correctly' perform femininity.[46] These narratives concern class as much as gender, from the lauding of Cheryl Cole as a 'chav' scrubbed up and made good, to the double-edged lamentations for Amy Winehouse as an unrepentant 'chav' whose bad-girl recklessness and self-indulgence led her to an early exit, to Adele's celebration as a tamely outspoken and 'classy' anti-chav.

The evolution of teenage Tyneside waitress Cheryl Tweedy into Cheryl Cole, like that of Posh Spice into Victoria Beckham, was a strictly managed and directed fairytale. Her 'amazing transformation', as a suspicious *Daily Mail* headline put it, 'from working-class convict to A-list celebrity' involved the ironing out of a 'tough' and 'sullen' personality, conveyed by 'before'

photographs of Cole displaying well-established chavette signifiers including gold hoop earrings, tracksuits and a scraped
back ponytail. The headline made clear how remarkable, if not
unthinkable, any elision of the two categories could be.
Extracted from her council estate and comprehensive-schooled
beginnings, Cole's rise to fame with the staunchly manufactured
Girls Aloud was presented as redemptive rescue from a class
again defined not by occupation but by cultural association with
the criminal and immoral (a 2012 biography of Tulisa
Contostavlos similarly presented her as 'a girl determined to
leave behind a life [of] underage sex, smoking weed, drinking
cider... to find her redemption with N-Dubz'). The initial
marketing of Girls Aloud, however, particularly their debut
Sound of the Underground, drew on the perceived edginess of
their class identity in an attempt to grant them a measure of
credibility, almost certainly in response to the similarly
successful packaging of contemporaries like Sugababes. In 2006,
a Girls Aloud set at Wembley Arena included an awkwardly
impressive cover of the Kaiser Chiefs' I Predict a Riot. Their
reclamatory performance imbued with gleeful menace and
evoking a scrappy populist solidarity, Girls Aloud occupy the
song's territory rather than joining Ricky Wilson in fleeing it, the
potential riot regarded not with fear but with a rush of antici-
patory adrenaline.

From these relatively auspicious beginnings, Cole's music
dwindled to indolent, autotuned dreck as her 'nation's sweet-
heart' stock rose. Embarking on a solo career in 2008, with little
secret made of her reliance on songwriters, session musicians
and stage-management, Cole's subsequent celebrity has hinged
less on her music than on what she represents: a 'regular girl'
plucked from regional obscurity for international acclaim, and,
after her short-lived marriage had cemented her fame, a
righteous wronged woman whose public catharsis was played
out in songs into which, despite their peppering with references

to love fought for, hard-won and lost, she had almost no creative input. Her 'regular girl' status is also a fetish, her background, style and accent mockingly exoticised in order to emphasise the incongruity of someone of her class on the national stage (see the Twitter account @CherylKerl and similar exercises in regional minstrelsy). While a charitable counter-reading of Cole's fame might applaud her as a role model for women escaping class disadvantage and dysfunctional relationships, her hegemonic usefulness lies in her status as a post-Diana 'peoples' princess', celebrated for the ability to turn a profit but never allowed to forget how constrained she remains by the background by whose distance her success is measured. The advancing shutdown of social mobility goes hand in hand with the idea of a change in class status as something bestowed upon working-class women as if by magic, an arbitrary gift gained by adherence to standards of beauty and behaviour rather than merit, in exchange for a willingness to be manufactured out of all recognition. Cole is presented as a fortunate serf turned Lady Bountiful, the Cheryl Cole Foundation auctioning her dresses to philanthropically plough the proceeds into her native North East, but she remains harried at every turn by media pronounce-ments on her body, dress and behaviour, endlessly policed for any sign of vulgarity, for a class-inflected idea of glamour which her betters might read as 'chavvy', as did the designer Julien Macdonald in 2010, chiding Cole for her ill-advised subscription to highstreet fashion. One wrong step towards the 'cheap and tacky' and, like Cinderella at the stroke of midnight, Cole could find herself transformed into Jade Goody or Kerry Katona, slumping back into the contemptible drain-circling chavdom from which the princely advances of Simon Cowell and Xenomania had seen her rescued. We are a long way from the stylish independence and insouciant self-expression of Kenickie.

Camden's late *mater dolorosa* Amy Winehouse, meanwhile, for all the typically Machiavellian marketing which surrounded her career, was an unlikely star to launch even before the drink, drugs, bisexuality, tattoos, self-harm and sprawling domestic disharmony set in. 2003 was a year of slickly manufactured, crowdpleasing pop anthems spawned by reality TV or established industry hit machines, including Cheryl Cole's early success with Girls Aloud. Within this picture, Winehouse's reinvigorated vintage soul and jazz, subtly powerful and bleakly explicit, felt like grit among gloss. The definitive and self-mythologising 2006 single Rehab, like much of her material, addresses addiction, dependency, depression and the complexities of female independence with a wry and self-aware wit that could have leavened the weight of many a 90s confessional memoir. The posthumous tributes to Winehouse clotting the front pages in August 2011, though, reflect the more significant aspect of her fame: the purpose she served as media cipher. The narrative into which Winehouse was corralled – discovered, lauded, rewarded, exploited, drug-ravaged and wrung dry by the cynics and sycophants around her – has been a traditional trajectory for women in the public eye from Marilyn Monroe to Britney Spears. Mixed in with this, and with the additional clichés of the demon-driven artist, Winehouse's dedication to the life of a good-time girl, unashamedly embarked on a Night Out without end, provided an irresistible opportunity for the media to squeeze the shapeless and slippery business of living into a rigid mould of meaning, to make her a signifier of the plagues afflicting modern womanhood; not all of modern womanhood, of course, just those of us susceptible to the lure of urban independence and its giddy, glittering thrills. The media's concentration on her as a reliably scandalous page-filler embedded her in public consciousness not as an artist but as a cautionary tale, eliciting a strange and volatile mixture of compassion and contempt. There was, too, a ghoulish and lascivious edge to public concern over Winehouse seldom present in attitudes to her male counterparts; her fellow crack cocaine aficionado Peter Doherty, to take the obvious contemporary example, was as lauded for his 'superlad' reckless dissipation as he was condemned. Following her death, the same organs which engorged themselves with pictures of Winehouse in her various stages of decline, distress and debauchery continued to objectify and sensationalise her as, inevitably, a 'brilliant but troubled' combination of tragic loss and dreadful warning. Amy Winehouse deserves a better class of memorialist, but her didactic usefulness in life and death is clear.

Winehouse's second album *Back to Black*, with its international success and clutch of awards, as well as the sheer depth of its influence, began a scramble by record companies to scrounge up similar eclectic and experimental women artists, triggering an exoticised and largely indistinguishable female-centred quirk-quake: Little Pixie Roux and the Machine for Lashes. It also got us Adele, who purveys a cleaned-up version of Winehouse's musical style, and who in 2011 was thrown into the vanguard of another putative Real Women in Music revolution when the head of her record label, Richard Russell, decreed that she exemplified everything healthy and hopeful in the otherwise dire and overheated state of contemporary music:

> The whole message with [Adele] is that it's just music, it's just really good music. There is nothing else. There are no gimmicks, no selling of sexuality. I think in the American market, particularly, they have come to the conclusion that is what you have to do.[47]

The 'just really good music' school of promotion employed here echoes the defence of post-Oasis lad rock, in its focus on technical aptitude to excuse its otherwise workmanlike and derivative quality. Adele's image is hardly free of contrivance, harking back as it does to the blue-eyed soul divas of the 1960s, 'classily' sexualised, perhaps, but sexualised nonetheless. In her chosen brand of popular music, a degree of sex in one's self-presentation is, as Russell correctly identifies, inextricably linked to commercial success. One could even argue, unfortunately, that it is Adele's very distance from the currently acceptable aesthetic norms of her genre that requires her to be marketed with a different, 'desexualised' focus. Had Adele possessed her own voice but the body of, oh, let's say Katy Perry, would her image and marketing have been sexed-up business as usual? The 'classy' aspect of Adele's presentation is of course also informed by prevailing ideas of appropriate feminine appearance and deportment: you wouldn't catch Adele in anything from Kenickie's 'cheap and tacky' dressing-up box, or throwing up her kebab alongside Shampoo. The assertion of a regulated femininity, defined against the lack of taste, 'vulgarity' or 'tartiness' now increasingly conflated with 'chav', with one feminine identity approved of and the other condemned, is problematic in the qualities it seeks to assign to 'real women'. Russell additionally claims that Adele's refusal to bow to a blandly beautiful industry standard is as radical today as the Prodigy were in the early 90s – never mind that the Prodigy were highly politicised and engaged with a wider oppositional culture, while Adele has been most outspoken in bemoaning her financial burden as a higher-rate taxpayer. That she can be said to occupy a radical position is more an indictment of the colourless state of contemporary music than it is a compliment to her. Despite her marketing and frequent reception as a 'real' representative of her gender and class, and for all her undoubted talent and likeability, Adele's 'radicalism' is about as straightforwardly progressive as the idea of Thatcher as the original Spice Girl.

PART THREE:
WHAT KIND OF A-TO-Z WOULD
GET YOU HERE?

'You know, if the Prime Minister wants to come to your fucking place, it's your fucking civic duty to welcome him'.
- Alex James (Blur), 2012

Privilege plays pop

If 90s indie was the setting for a spectacular cultural coup by the forces of neoliberalism, 00s indie was their victory parade. This has been nowhere more evident than in indie's lack of engagement with an increasingly blatant rightward drift in British politics and society, which one might have expected to produce some regrouping or revival of the counterculture, but to which opposition has been half-hearted at best. Indie's choking off as a source of oppositional energy has some obvious points of culpability, namely the filleting of the independent sector itself and the narrowing of access to the arts for unfunded and unconnected hopefuls. The concordance of both has resulted in the much-discussed grotesquery whereby the majority of British chart acts are now either privately educated or from prestigious stage schools. This diagnosis was made by *The Word* magazine in December 2010, in a piece which established that 60% of British artists in a recent UK top 10 had been to public school, compared with 20% in 1990. Expressions of disquiet over this generated several predictable red-herring discussions on the absurdity of arguing that comprehensive-schooled musicians automatically made good music and privately schooled musicians automatically bad, which hardly anyone has actually argued in this connection.[48] The issue is less the presence of public school boys and girls in music, whether Joe Strummer or Jack Peñate, and more the marked material advantage which aspirant musicians are now granted by their background.

You don't have to be backed by family wealth and a private education to make it big in British music today, but it certainly helps. Currently, the ability to embark upon a potentially less than lucrative artistic career is assisted immensely by the support of affluent parents, trust funds or inheritances, which can provide equipment, studio time, venue hire and publicity, in addition to the relative peace of mind secured by financial stability which is often a prerequisite for immersion in creative work. Having parents who take care of rent can also allow one to live, network and play in the same prohibitively-priced milieu as one's professional peers, a process which can also be considerably aided by contacts made at school or university. For those of us with no such financial safety-net, creative and entre-preneurial risk-taking becomes far more of a luxury. Young people with artistic ambition but modest means, with no other form of support than their own capacity and tolerance for paid labour, find it accordingly harder to devote time and energy to creative endeavours, especially in circumstances where the already scant chances of surviving as an artist on the dole are now vanishing. The current climate bears instructive comparison with the late 70s and early 80s, when many post-punk bands, for instance, were able to construct an independent and experimentalist subcultural alternative, facilitated by an abundance of collective living spaces and the relative munifi-cence, at £40 each week, of the Enterprise Allowance. This phase of creative development is increasingly open only to those who can afford to live or work in the now gentrified locations of these former art-squats and community spaces. Mainstream success is increasingly predicated on a band having sufficient money and contacts to supply the panicky, risk-averse and short-termist demands of the music industry, and the capacity to be 'pre-marketed' through their own resources, publicity and contacts, which again disadvantages artists without the background to secure these.

Noah & The Whale's frontman Charlie Fink, a graduate of St Paul's school along with John Milton, Sir Isaiah Berlin and the present Chancellor of the Exchequer, has rejected the idea – admittedly misconceived, but also very infrequently expressed – that a private school education automatically makes for bad art, saying: 'I don't think with our songs where we come from really comes into it, because it's rare that we write about it'.[49] Well, quite. Beneficiaries of privilege are prone to take many things for granted, including the nature of their own success, which they are understandably inclined to attribute more to merit and graft than to the types of structural advantage outlined above. This is not to suggest that their success is undeserved, but their resultant lack of experience of endemic disadvantage can diminish the likelihood of their examining their circumstances, much less questioning or challenging them. There has always been a place for the posh in music, and there has always been a tolerance of their tendency to play pantomime proles. What we have seen in the last decade or so is not a takeover by one side, but a vanishing of the other, and, with the restriction of working-class access to politics, media and the arts – Red Toryism's architect Phillip Blond, no less, notes that the UK currently has one of the lowest rates of social mobility in the developed world – the predominance of the privileged has become more glaring.[50] It is the unexamined colonising of popular music by privately educated and stage-schooled careerists, coupled with the decline in access and influence among those of a less privileged background, who have come to be represented overwhelmingly by negative or comical stereotypes, which has commentators troubled, along with the accompanying uncoupling of 'indie' from the politics which formerly distinguished at least part of it.

The strange death of radical indie

While indie has very visibly slipped from diversity informed by political engagement to homogeneity characterised by political disengagement, alarming levels of tedium, tameness and sameness are hardly confined to contemporary music. 00s popular culture in general was defined by a peculiar resistance to novelty, with entertainment retreating down the cultural cul-de-sacs of reality TV or remakes and rebrandings of the already bankable, safe and commodified: jukebox musicals, the filming of superannuated Tolkien canon or J. K. Rowling's Blytonesque confections. Caution and cynicism became creative watchwords on page, stage and screen. But in popular music, what the critic Simon Reynolds has diagnosed as 'retromania' seemed particularly pervasive, from the proliferation of reformed bands and tribute acts to the turbo-charged recycling of previous trends. Mark Fisher has analysed retromania as a function of what he characterises as the 'capitalist realist' aspect of neoliberalism: the stifling of innovation through the denial of any possible future fundamentally different from the present. Reflecting on the fact that:

> There just doesn't seem to be any music which has substantially grasped the new mood after 2010 really in this country. It seems to me to be a major disjunction between the political situation and cultural forms. The cultural forms that dominate still seem to be so pre-2008 actually... Politics is ahead and culture hasn't caught up with it...[51]

Fisher concludes that capitalist realism can be situated as a 'kind of naturalised postmodernism' involving 'increased reliance on existing forms, pastiche and retrospection'. Whether one views capitalist realism as a motor of retromania, or as an explanation of the creative dearth resulting from less conscious social processes, this observation has obvious resonances with the *j'accuse* directed by Douglas Haddow at 00s hipster culture, its appetite for the ironic appropriation of previous cultural signifiers having neutered its potential for radicalism and innovation:

> *An artificial appropriation of different styles from different eras, the hipster represents the end of Western civilization – a culture lost in the superficiality of its past and unable to create any new meaning. Not only is it unsustainable, it is suicidal. While previous youth movements have challenged the dysfunction and decadence of their elders, today we have the 'hipster' – a youth subculture that mirrors the doomed shallowness of mainstream society.*[52]

Maybe all those zeroes should have been a clue. The 00s began as a blank slate, supposedly wiped clean of the messily complex scribbles that defined the previous era. The twentieth century's closing scenes having witnessed the apparent end of history rather begged the question of what on earth we were meant to do from now on. The same instability and uncertainty which has produced a loss of faith in political orthodoxies, and analytical paralysis in the face of a multiplicity of alternatives, has also produced a splintered and disintegrated culture at a loss as to how to define itself and, given the apparent imminence of disaster, unconvinced that it's worthwhile bothering to do so. We have fallen back on imitations or wholesale reproductions of the tried, tested and tired-out because creating or producing anything culturally distinctive currently seems as pressing and productive a task as arranging deckchairs in a previously untried aesthetically pleasing pattern on the Titanic.

The fault for this impasse can no more be laid at the feet of Oasis, or Ricky Wilson, or Adele, or even Alex James, than one can blame a litter of puppies for pissing on a heap of abandoned newspapers. Just as Britpop's decline and fall was tied to the demands of hype and branding and product, so the bland and stultified homogeneity which has made contemporary music the source of such comprehensive complaint: its built-in obsolescence, its staleness and disposability, illustrates the acquiescence of pop culture to neoliberalism's 'end of history' propaganda. Following the 90s triumph of irony, and intensification in signifiers stripped of meaning, the 00s acceleration and consolidation of retromania oversaw not merely the predictable co-option of previously subversive movements, from second-wave Britpop's attenuation of post-punk's radicalism and innovation, to the compromised conservatism of nu-folk, but their co-option to the extent of preventing the emergence of anything new. At the nadir of this downward spiral, a song like Sandi Thom's 2006 I Wish I Was a Punk Rocker (With Flowers in my Hair), a dazzlingly superficial paean to 60s and 70s 'authenticity' which also simplifies and reduces the signifiers of these past identities to fashion accessories, seemed to simultaneously commodify and celebrate the death of meaningful traditions, and, in its odd conflation of punk and hippy signifiers, it wilfully confused even that which it claimed to care about. There has always been 'posh' music, and there has always been manufactured music, but add to this the Britpop-led destruction of the independent sector in pursuit of careerist and commercial imperatives; the resultant industry hostility towards the new, untried and perhaps unprofitable; the retromanic reliance on resuscitating previous forms at the expense of innovation; and the social stratification of access to the arts and entertainment sector; and you have the apparently terminal decline of conditions which ensured that more interesting, experimental, and oppositional music was both created and heard.

Let them eat cupcakes

Throughout the 00s, commodification of the culture of the poor moved – or indeed reverted – from the urban and post-industrial to the rural and domestic. Alex Niven's *Folk Opposition* (2011) argued that the genre of nu-folk, in particular, accords more with the perspective of an elitist political establishment than with popular sentiment. David Cameron's appreciation for nu-folk artists, including Mumford & Sons and Gillian Welch, is as much an indicator of hegemony as was Blair's grasping of the coattails of Britpop's rising stars. One of the functions of nu-folk, as with other folk-inflected lifestyle trends (artisan bread, peasant-style smocks, flea-marketeering) is to garb its adherents in a whimsically imagined 'common culture', bestowing credibility through association with an edgily authentic 'folk' identity. This trend in its first flushes was, crucially, an expensive lifestyle choice to manage and sustain, hence its aspirational appeal. Some irony lay in the trend's lack of accessibility to those whose stereotyped and idealised nature (the authenticity, simplicity and uncorrupted innocence associated with closeness to nature and distance from wealth) it sought to appropriate, as well as in the trend's enthusiasts paying through the nose for products valued according to how closely they approximated the simple, the natural, and the freely available.

More recently, it has been possible to detect an insidious intertwining of this cultural predilection for a kind of atavistic Puritanism in food, clothing and décor with the Coalition's rhetoric of austerity. 'Austerity chic' fits comfortably within the construction of a stoical and resolute 'British' identity, as exemplified by the creepy ubiquity of Keep Calm and Carry On, a motif redolent of a previous time of enforced austerity and international instability which few of us experienced as anything more than vintage-chic, but from which 'we' know that 'we' emerged victorious. However, it also serves to license increased authoritarianism and prescription in the arena of social policy, where it is assisted by the rhetoric of 'scroungers' and 'chavs'. Austerity chic entails the fatalistic acceptance of austerity rhetoric, often swallowed with the sugary conceit that austerity is a righteous burden the nation must dutifully shoulder – rather than something imposed from above as a consequence of the corruption and incompetence of a financial elite – along with a smugly puritanical anticipation of exhibiting this righteous submission to economic hardship through one's consumer choices. Lifestyle supplements which showcase high-end restaurants where dishes using 'poverty cuts' of meat can be sampled, or 'poverty cookbooks' in which a fetish is made of techniques and ingredients historically used through necessity rather than choice, sit awkwardly next to sensationalist reporting on the malnutrition often typical of life on a low income.[53] But the latter demographic, of course, are presented and received as 'chavs', in opposition to those righteously and regretfully having to tighten their belts. The irresponsible and undeserving poor's alleged diet of chips and lager rather than honourably simple and highly-priced artisan bread, and alleged profligate spending on vulgar and flashy consumer goods (trainers, plasma screen TVs) or on vices (drugs, junk food, gambling), is enough to condemn them out of hand. This enforced narrative of vice against virtue functions, again, as both a method of differentiating classes and a means of explaining their subsequent predicament, regardless of the relation this bears to reality.

This conflating of material and moral poverty aligns neatly with the attempted construction of a similar hegemonic concordance to that which took place around Britpop, once again based on 'branding the nation'. The 2012 Diamond Jubilee and Olympic Games featured an intrusive amount of union flag branding, not least when compared with the muted Golden

Jubilee celebrations in 2002. The decade since then has witnessed the return of many anxieties repressed or soothed by the 90s boom, which have incurred a greater preoccupation with irresolvable but distracting debates on national identity and social cohesion. Whereas Blair offered disingenuous and shallow optimism as balm for economic ills, Cameron, at the head of a government distanced by birth, wealth and schooling from the majority of society, can offer only savage Hobbesian pessimism which plays out in the stereotyping and demonizing of various sections of society who cannot or will not fit within the national pale. In addition to the imaginative rebranding of the underprivileged as undeserving 'chavs', the Coalition's class warfare has taken place against a background of unapologetically aristocratic and paternalist motifs: the lush vistas of *Downton Abbey*, remakes of *Upstairs Downstairs* and *Titanic*, and the unironic adoption of Barbour jackets and tweed on the catwalk. Slotting neatly into the retromanic vogue for taking refuge in the past, this nostalgic romanticism of social stratification, of deference, of a 'respectable' hard work ethic for the many and fashionable indolence for the few, takes place against the bizarro-world backdrop of young people being asked to undertake unpaid work placements under threat of losing their benefits, with refusal to do so inviting accusations of being a 'job snob'. It is the return of the rhetoric of justified hierarchy, of not thinking you're too good for what you're given, of not only knowing your place but accepting it with deferent, meek and even grateful compliance.

Radical chav: we are all underclass now?

Over the past decade, the innovative and the oppositional impulse in UK music have been far less evident in traditional guitar rock than in elements of hip-hop and particularly of grime – an offshoot of what Simon Reynolds describes as 'the hardcore continuum', rooted in East London's council estates and in DIY networks of production, transmission and distribution, idiosyncratically British, multiracial and with a small but significant female presence. The Metropolitan Police's Form 696, assessing the risks of holding live music events in the capital, focused specifically on the organisation and promotion of hip-hop and grime nights in a more overtly discriminatory echo of the 'repetitive beats' clause of the Criminal Justice Bill.[54] In this context, it's perhaps unsurprising that the most talked-about musical critique of the Coalition emerged not from indie but from this musical *milieu*, and from an unironic acceptance of the 'chav' identity frequently associated with it. In March 2012 Plan B, an Albarnesque polymath and dilettante who had followed his hip-hop debut with an album of post-Winehouse soul, released Ill Manors, a single widely touted as a bone thrown to those of us starved of contemporary protest songs.

The media response to the song tended to present Plan B as an authentic 'voice of the streets'; although he shares with both Mike Skinner and mid-period Doherty a certain wide-boy aesthetic which fed into his categorisation as 'chav', Plan B's 'liminal' upbringing ('We weren't working class but we weren't middle class, we were in the void in-between') places him closer to someone like Jarvis Cocker on the spectrum of tenuous working-class heroism.[55] Tied to debates around the riots of August 2011, the video accompanying Ill Manors juxtaposed a cartoony burlesque of inner-city violence with the public-record violence of police and government representatives, questioning the distinctions between them in the same way that the Manic Street Preachers' censored video for Design for Life had in 1996. On one level as pantomime as Girls Aloud covering I Predict a Riot, and building to an exhilarating rich-boy baiting chorus as reductive, lurid and essentialist as (I Want to) Kill Somebody, against its sampled swoop of agitated strings Ill Manors offered more depth than either in its lyrical critique of the immediate origins of the present crisis: cuts to youth and community facilities, the disingenuousness and missed opportunities of London's pre-Olympics regeneration, and media and government demonisation of the young multiracial poor. Ill Manors did not recoil from potentially embarrassing earnestness, nor from allying itself in sound, aesthetic and lyrical content with 'council estate kids', hoodies, gangs, and all the great panic-inducing panoply of chav-land. Most strikingly, the song consciously takes on an externally imposed, despised 'underclass' identity in order to suggest that identity's potential for radical opposition. In place of Design for Life's embittered elegy for a defeated proletariat, or the time-biding and, ultimately, nonviolent revenge fantasy of Mis-Shapes, Ill Manors uses the power of hegemonic class narratives to imbue itself with something close to genuine threat. The chorused 'Don't come round here no more' resounds as a concluding, blackly comic riposte to the past few decades, offering to actively put an end to the class tourism which Common People merely critiqued, in a carnivalesque inversion of norms in which the lower orders instruct the agents of gentrification, tourism and voyeurism to get off our land under threat of being engaged with 'for real'. The appropriative, objectifying middle-class fantasy of underclass violence, anger and resentment is taken at face value and made retaliatory flesh, vivid and livid.

Does the potential for oppositional chav-pop make it possible to view the 'chav' identity itself as a logical and appropriate response to current conditions? Something seemingly overlooked in the past few years' constant referencing of a 'lost generation' and of 'graduates without a future' was that, lower down the socioeconomic scale, little had substantially changed. For many with memories that stretch beyond the credit crunch, the last recession and the last UK election, attaining comfort and security has always been a struggle, and home ownership or independently funded internships, for instance, have always seemed implausible if not impossible. Simmering but unspoken discontent, alienation, anomie and lacking signs of positive change have been a way of life to which many have of necessity had to reconcile ourselves, not a sign of the final crisis or a spur to mounting the barricades. For many there has always been poverty, precarity, petty criminality and police animosity, but the years since the crisis of 2008 have exacerbated their reach and increased their visibility, resulting in their sudden horrified pointing out by those who might previously have missed them due to being shielded by better prospects and broader horizons. At the same time, under the Coalition, the demise of upwards aspiration and social mobility, and the doublethink, delusion or deceit involved in the assertion of classlessness, have put an end to the affirmative, if blithely ignorant, appropriation of working-class signifiers which was encouraged in the Blair years. Now that things are going badly, poor is no longer cool, merely comical or contemptible.

As inequality and social immobility become harder to ignore, class is regaining both meaning and power, and, in order to deal with this, gradations of inter-class status are attaining greater importance as ways of assuaging resentment and asserting superiority. Consciousness of class is resurgent, on the one hand, in the increased visibility of 'chav' as mocked and feared other in both politics and pop culture, and on the other, in the increased unironically expressed admiration for 'posh' signifiers. As austerity continues to clamp down, however, with more jobs lost, more wages cut, more benefits denied and more state services eroded, class and indeed 'chav' identity and consciousness may be subject to shifting definitions and allegiances, with far more of us categorised by those above us as the workless, scrounging other, our latent 'chav' potential exposed. During this process, in which more of us find ourselves on the wrong side of the division between judging and judged, coming to see the poor from within and not without, the exaggerations, misinformation and lies employed in the demonisation of this demographic may become evident and this particular politicised stereotype may be questioned, qualified and challenged until it dissolves.

There are manifold dangers in responding to any such development by asserting exclusionary models of alternative, 'authentic' working-class identity, which ignore or sentimentalise aspects of the past and present, and which obscure the presence of multivalent working-class identities: female, multiracial, queer, aesthetes and autodidacts as well as 'chavs'. Instead, challenges to the 'chav' identity, especially as that category expands and diversifies under austerity, should also challenge the idea of a strictly homogenous 'working class' coded as white and masculine, thereby creating the potential for solidarity on a broader front. Class identity is a constantly shifting response to historical conditions, an ongoing production rather than a finished product. Constructive approaches to working-class representation should not fall prey to the same nostalgic and romanticised construction of national identity which informed Cool Britannia as much as Blue Labour – and as much as Ed Miliband's mugging of Disraeli for his 'One Nation' 2012 conference speech – but rather engage with what they find as they find it, if necessary taking ownership of externally-imposed narratives, occupying them, inverting them.

The Victoria & Albert Museum's 2012 retrospective on British design claimed, with a familiar note of wishful thinking, that times of austerity in Britain have also been moments of creative renewal, noting artistic excitement during the postwar period, the 70s oil crisis, and the recession of the 80s. One need not be a victim of rose-tinted personal nostalgia to argue that popular culture seems currently consumed by pastiche, recycling, solipsistic navel-gazing and pantomimes of authenticity, preoccupied with kitsch fripperies and politically disengaged, with previous traditions of protest and consciousness weakened, compromised, commodified, confused or forgotten. Pop-cultural representations of the working class, in particular, have become so thin, so shallow, repetitive and unimaginative, that they do us all a disservice. An injection of new imagination, borne of diverse and unacknowledged experiences, is necessary if we are to slip the coils of political regression and artistic monotony. This experience will be informed by knowledge that the game is rigged, that what attempts at meritocracy and amelioration once existed are now being systematically rolled back, that application and talent do not automatically enable one to rise, and that the current likely alternative to dissolute idleness is not industrious and productive respectable labour but immiserating and precarious toil for inadequate remuneration. From this perspective, immersion in the alternatives offered by what we are told are vulgar 'chav' values – the Night Out, excess, hedonism, short-term enjoyment, glamour and sex and substance use and the radical possibilities of pleasure – looks less like a moral panic and more like a moral imperative. Successive generations have surely educated, agitated and organised for more than the opportunity to dutifully spend our diminished wages on an austerity-chic cookbook.

Notes

1. See http://www.standard.co.uk/lifestyle/london-life/politics-is-not-my-thing—but-i-was-delighted-when-the-camerons-came-to-my-farm-7546696.html. On 'the arseoisie', see Marina Hyde, 'Alex James's new memoir proves him to be Britain's premier cheese bore', accessed July 2012 at http://www.guardian.co.uk/lifeandstyle/lostinshowbiz/2012/feb/16/alex-james-memoir-cheese

2. Stuart Hall (2011), 'The neoliberal revolution', *Soundings* 48 (Summer 2011), pp.9-28

3. Imogen Tyler, 'Chav Mum, Chav Scum: Class Disgust in Contemporary Britain', *Feminist Media Studies* 8:2 (June 2008)

4. C Beatty, S Fothergill and R Powell (2007), 'Twenty Years On: Has the Economy of the Coalfields Recovered?', Centre for Regional Economic and Social Research, Sheffield Hallam University. Published in *Environment and Planning* A 39 (7), pp.1654-75.

5. See, for instance, http://www.dailymail.co.uk/news/article-2165757/Voters-Cameron-s-strip-child-benefit-workshy-parents.html, http://www.express.co.uk/posts/view/328808/Cameron-s-war-on-welfare-Jobless-couples-with-more-than-3-children-face-benefits-cull—Cameron-s-war-on-welfare-Jobless-couples-with-more-than-3-children-face-benefits-cull, http://www.huffingtonpost.co.uk/2012/06/25/cameron-housing-benefit-under-25s-child-benefit_n_1623238.html, all accessed July 2012

6. Stuart Hall *et al, Policing the Crisis: Mugging, the State and Law and Order* (1978)

7. Stanley Cohen, *Folk Devils and Moral Panics* (1972)

8. Peter Watson, 'From sharks to Shrek, we're all toothless now', *Times*, 14 July 2012

9. James Delingpole, 'A conspiracy against chavs? Count me in',

Times, 13 April 2006

10. See http://www.nytimes.com/2011/09/28/world/europe/ 28iht-letter28.html, accessed July 2012

11. See Diane Elson, 'The Economic, the Political and the Domestic: Businesses, States and Households in the Organisation of Production', *New Political Economy* 3:2 (1998), pp.189-208

12. See Beverley Skeggs, 'Classifying Practices: Representations, Capitals and Recognitions', in Pat Mahony and Christine Zmroczek (eds), *Class Matters: 'Working-Class' Women's Perspectives on Social Class* (1997)

13. See http://www.express.co.uk/ourcomments/view/122089/ Peter-Lilley-was-reviled-for-what-he-said-but-he-was-right, accessed August 2012

14. See Rhian E. Jones, 'Is 'Chav' a Feminist Issue?' at http:/ /www.badreputation.org.uk/2011/08/30/is-chav-a-feminist-issue; Ciara O'Connor, 'Chav-shaming' at http://www.thef word.org.uk/blog/2012/03/ciara_oconnor_d, both accessed August 2012

15. Pavan Amara, 'Feminism: Still excluding working-class women?', accessed August 2012 at http://www.thefwor d.org.uk/features/2012/03/feminism_still_.

16. See, for instance, Nina Power, *One Dimensional Woman* (2009); http://www.newleftproject.org/index.php/site/articl e_comments/when_austerity_sounds_like_backlash_gender _and_the_economic_crisis, accessed September 2012

17. See Imogen Tyler (2006), 'Chav Scum: the Filthy Politics of Social Class in Contemporary Britain', *M/C Journal* 9:5 (2006), accessed July 2012 at http://journal.media-cult ure.org.au/0610/09-tyler.php

18. The peculiar and frequently disturbing moral atmosphere of the early 1990s is precisely anatomised at: http://upclose-maspersonal.blogspot.co.uk/2012/07/haruspex-93.html

19. See, for instance, Carl Neville, *Classless* (2010), Paul Dave,

Visions of England: Class and Culture in Contemporary Cinema (2006), Julian Stallabrass, *High Art Lite* (2000)

20. John Beynon, *Masculinities and Culture* (2002)
21. *NME*, 16 September 1995
22. *Observer*, 17 September 1995
23. Not that the Manics' glam ambiguity or feminist sloganeering automatically implied enlightened attitudes in practice; *viz*. Barbara Ellen's account of their 1994 tour where 'laddishness' in full tedious swing – boozing and boorishness in Thailand's go-go bars – was self-consciously and somewhat sheepishly equated with being 'a brainless idiot' (Barbara Ellen (1994), 'Siamese Animal Men', accessed July 2012 at http://www.thisisyesterday.com/ints/bangkokint .html)
24. See Owen Hatherley, *Uncommon* (2011)
25. See http://www.thebeatjuice.com/interviews/view/518/1/ brett-anderson, accessed August 2012
26. See http://www.guardian.co.uk/politics/2012/jun/17/dennis-skinner-formed-pits-war, accessed August 2012
27. *NME Student Guide* (1993), accessed July 2012 at http://www.angelfire.com/rock2/suicideispainless/student-guide.html
28. See http://www.npr.org/blogs/monitormix/2009/11/swagger _like_us_thoughts_on_wo_2.html, accessed July 2012
29. Rebecca C. Hains (2009), 'Power Feminism, Mediated: Girl power and the commercial politics of change', *Women's Studies in Communication* 32:1 (2009), pp.89-113, p.98
30. See Natasha Walter, *The New Feminism* (1998). I have given a less laudatory analysis of Thatcher's image at: http://www. badreputation.org.uk/2012/01/10/on-thatcher-icons-and-iron-ladies-rhian-jones/
31. See http://www.monkeysyndicate.co.uk/chavspotting/chav history001.html, accessed August 2012.
32. See http://www.guardian.co.uk/artanddesign/2002/jul/06/ar

tsfeatures.features2, accessed August 2012

35. See http://reynoldsretro.blogspot.co.uk/2007_09_01_archive
.html, accessed August 2012

34. See John Harris, *The Last Party: Britpop, Blair and the Demise of English Rock* (2003), p.257-8, p.236, p.365

35. See *Deadline* magazine, quoted at http://pussyrockfan
zine.blogspot.co.uk/2010/11/article-review-shampoo-we-
are-shampoo.html, accessed September 2012

36. Although I vividly remember reading this line in a review of Kenickie, almost certainly in *Melody Maker* or *NME*, I have been unable to establish its author.

37-9. See http://www.gold.ac.uk/media/1iss6.pdf, with thanks to Emma Jackson for permission to quote.

40. Carol Dyhouse, *Glamour: Women, History, Feminism* (2011)

41. See http://www.guardian.co.uk/music/2006/apr/22/popan-
drock.libertines, accessed August 2012

42. See, for instance, http://www.guardian.co.uk/discussion
/comment-permalink/16925183, accessed July 2012

43. Beverley Skeggs (2001), 'The Toilet Paper: Femininity, Class and Misrecognition', Women's Studies International Forum. 24, (2-3): pp. 295-307, quoted in Imogen Tyler, 'Celebrity Chav: Fame, Femininity and Social Class' Draft, published by the Department of Sociology, Lancaster University, Lancaster LA1 4YT, UK at http://www.lancs.ac.uk/fass
/sociology/papers/tyler-whitetrashcelebrity.pdf

44. See http://version2.andrewkendall.com/pages/published/m
agazines/showpage/23/, accessed August 2012

45. See, for some of the issues surrounding 'domestic chic':
http://thequietus.com/articles/07962-cupcake-feminism,
accessed September 2012

46. Tyler, 'Celebrity Chav' Draft, at http://www.lancs.ac.uk/fass
/sociology/papers/tyler-whitetrashcelebrity.pdf

47. See http://www.guardian.co.uk/music/2011/may/29/adele-
change-women-music-business, accessed July 2012

48. http://news.bbc.co.uk/today/hi/today/newsid_9373000/9
373158.stm; see also http://www.guardian.co.uk/music/2007
/jul/08/popandrock, http://www.guardian.co.uk/music/musi
cblog/2007/jul/08/wewontheindiewarsbutatw, all accessed
August 2012

49. See http://news.bbc.co.uk/today/hi/today/newsid_9373000/9
373158.stm, accessed July 2012

50. See http://www.respublica.org.uk/item/England-s-Riotous-
Values; see also, for instance, http://www.suttontrust.com
/reports/Journalists-backgroundsfinal-report.pdf, accessed
August 2012

51. See http://www.newleftproject.org/index.php/site/print_ar
ticle/towards_a_new_hegemony, accessed July 2012

52. Douglas Haddow, 'Hipster: The Dead End of Western
Civilization', accessed August 2012 at http://www.adbus
ters.org/magazine/79/hipster.html

53. See, for instance, the *Observer* of 22 January 2012, in which
Rachel Cooke demonstrates a fatalistic acceptance of the rise
of austerity rhetoric – along with full awareness of its disingenuous nature – but nevertheless looks forward to the
revival of recession-chic in cookery (http://www.guardian
.co.uk/lifeandstyle/2012/jan/22/rachel-cooke-food-great-
depression); the same edition splashed on the ostensibly
shocking news that poorer families were, in a time of
enforced austerity, often less able or willing to spend money
on fruit and vegetables (http://www.guardian.co.uk/lifeand-
style/2012/jan/22/fruit-vegetable-consumption-poorer-
families).

54. See http://www.guardian.co.uk/commentisfree/2012/jan/10
/police-stigmatising-hip-hop-696-form, accessed September
2012

55. See http://www.guardian.co.uk/music/musicblog/2012/mar
/15/plan-b-ill-manors, accessed August 2012. The 'liminal
class', defined as lower-middle/upper-working class, is

clarified by Simon Reynolds at, for instance, http://www.furious.com/perfect/simonreynolds31.html, accessed September 2012.

Acknowledgements

Parts of this book began life on the blogs Velvet Coalmine, Bad Reputation, and Up Close and Personal.

For their various sorts of help in producing this book, I am grateful to: Pavan Amara, Sinead Mulready, Alex Niven, Imogen Tyler, James Ivens, 'Pere Lebrun', Amy Baldwin, Jacob Lloyd, Siân Neilson, Theresa Kanneh, Miranda Brennan, El Black, Ruth Prendecki, Linda, Robert and Emily Jones, and Sara, Ceri and Chris.